JUNIOR Dictionary

First published in 2016 by Miles Kelly Publishing Ltd
Harding's Barn, Bardfield End Green, Thaxted, Essex, CM6 3PX, UK

2 4 6 8 10 9 7 5 3 1

Publishing Director Belinda Gallagher
Creative Director Jo Cowan
Editors Carly Blake, Rosie Neave, Sarah Parkin
Editorial Assistant Lauren White
Cover Designer Simon Lee
Designers Jo Cowan, Kayleigh Allen
Production Elizabeth Collins, Caroline Kelly
Reprographics Stephan Davis, Jennifer Cozens, Thom Allaway

ISBN 978-1-78209-968-0

Printed in China

British Library Cataloguing-in-Publication Data
A catalogue record for this book is available from the British Library

Made with paper from a sustainable forest

www.mileskelly.net

JUNIOR Dictionary

Author and consultant
Susan Purcell

Miles
Kelly

How to use your dictionary

Cartoons

Look out for the fun cartoons that appear in each letter. How many different things can you see starting with the same letter?

Entries

*The words in **bold** are the entries, the words that you look up. There are more than 1700 entries in your dictionary.*

Definitions

These come after each entry. They explain what the word means.

Example sentences

A sentence follows each definition. This gives you an example of the word within a sentence.

a b c d e f g h i j k l m n o p q r s **t** u v w x y z

How many things can you spot beginning with 't'?

Tt

tadpole (tadpoles)
a very young frog or toad
Tadpoles have big heads and long tails and live in water.

tail (tails)
the part of an animal at the end of its back
The dog has a long, white tail.

tail

table (tables)
1 a piece of furniture with legs and a flat top
Please clear the table.
2 a list of numbers or words written in rows and columns
We measured the height of everyone in the class and wrote the results in a table.

take (taking, took, take
1 to carry something
Take an umbrella with you.
2 to move something or someone to another pla
Can you take us to the station?
3 to steal
The thieves took all the money.

Different forms of a word

Some entries are followed by the same word in plural form. This is when there is more than one of something. The plural is shown after the entry within brackets.

talent (talents)
the ability to do something very well without having to learn it
Maya has a talent for drawing.

talk (talking, talked)
to speak
We talked on the phone for ages.

tall
1 higher than normal
My grandad is tall, and I am short.
2 having a certain height
How tall are you?

tambourine (tambourines)
a small round musical instrument that you shake or hit
I played the tambourine in the school concert.

tank (tanks)
1 a container for liquids
There's a leak in the petrol tank.
2 a strong truck used by soldiers
Tanks have metal tracks or belts instead of wheels.

tap (taps)
something that controls the flow of a liquid or gas
Turn the tap off; don't waste water.

tape
a flat, narrow strip of plastic that is sticky on one side
Put some sticky tape on the envelope.

taste (tasting, tasted)
1 to have a flavour
What does the soup taste like?
2 to try a little food or drink to see what it is like
Have you tasted the pizza?

taxi (taxis)
a car that takes people to different places, for money
We'll take a taxi.

tea
1 a hot drink made from leaves
Do you take milk in your tea?
2 a meal you eat in the early evening
What's for tea?

teacher (teachers)
a person who gives lessons in a subject
Our teacher's name is Mrs Griffiths.

teacher

a b c d e f g h i j k l m n o p q r s **t** u v w x y z

Verbs

If an entry is a verb (doing word) then other forms of the word will appear in brackets. For example, the verb 'taste' is followed by different endings.

Alphabetical order

All of the entries are in alphabetical order. The alphabet is listed down the side of each page. Use the highlighted letters to help you find your way around.

Illustrations and photographs

These help you to understand the meaning of a word. Each illustration or photograph has its own label to tell you exactly what it is.

Puzzle time
These are fun things to do and give you a chance to play with words. This helps you to learn and remember them.

a
b
c
d
e
f
g
h
i
j
k
l
m
n
o
p
q
r
s
t
u
v
w
x
y
z

How many things can you spot beginning with 'a'?

A a

above
1 in a higher place than something else
Annie lives in the flat above us.
2 more than
This ride is for children aged six and above.

absent
away from a place, not there
Sameer is absent today.

accident (accidents)
1 an unexpected event, often causing damage or injury
There was an accident on the road.
2 something that happens by chance
I dropped it by accident.

actor (actress; actors, actresses)
a person who plays a part in a film or play
My Dad is an actor.

add

add (adding, added)
1 to put something together with something else
Add the milk and sugar to the butter.

2 to put numbers together to find the total

If you add six to four it makes ten.

address (addresses)

the house number and street where you live

My address is 65 Chestnut Avenue.

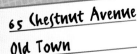

65 Chestnut Avenue

Old Town

Southshire

address

adult (adults)

a grown-up, not a child

Only adults are allowed in the pool after six p.m.

adult

adventure (adventures)

an exciting experience

Flying is such an adventure.

advert (advertisement; adverts, advertisements)

words or pictures in newspapers or on television about things for sale

There are too many adverts on TV.

aerial (aerials)

a piece of metal or wire for receiving or sending radio or television signals

There is an aerial on our roof.

aeroplane (aeroplanes)

a large machine, with wings and an engine, that flies

When aeroplanes fly over our house it is very noisy.

afraid

scared, frightened

Are you afraid of snakes?

afternoon (afternoons)

the part of the day between midday and the evening

We'll go out this afternoon.

again

another time, once more

Shall we sing the song again?

age

the number of years someone has lived

At what age can I learn to drive?

air

the mixture of gases around us that we breathe

The air is clean and fresh.

a b c d e f g h i j k l m n o p q r s t u v w x y z

a
b
c
d
e
f
g
h
i
j
k
l
m
n
o
p
q
r
s
t

aircraft (plural is the same)
machines that fly
Helicopters are a type of aircraft.

airport (airports)
a place where planes land and
take off
The airport is very busy today.

alarm (alarms)
a machine that flashes or makes
a noise as a warning
The burglar alarm is flashing!

alien (aliens)
something strange that comes
from another planet
E.T. is a friendly alien.

alligator (alligators)
a type of large reptile that looks
similar to a crocodile
*Alligators spend much of their day
in water, keeping cool and hidden
from view.*

alligator

alphabet (alphabets)
letters in a special order that
form a language
'E' is a letter of the alphabet.

ambulance (ambulances)
a vehicle for taking people to
and from hospital
Stop! There's an ambulance coming.

ambulance

anchor (anchors)
a heavy metal object on a rope or
chain, which stops a boat moving.
Lower the anchor.

angel (angels)
a messenger from God, in some
religions
In pictures, angels often have wings.

angry (angrier, angriest)
feeling or showing annoyance
My sister sometimes gets angry.

animal (animals)
a living thing that can move
Cows and horses are animals.

ankle (ankles)
the part of the body between the
leg and the foot
I twisted my ankle when I fell over.

answer (answers)
1 something you say or write
after a question
My answer is no.
2 the correct solution
Well done! That's the right answer.

answer (answering, answered)
1 to say or write something when
asked a question
*Where have you been? Please
answer my question.*
2 to pick up the telephone or go
to the door
Please answer the telephone.

ant (ants)
a tiny insect that lives in groups
Some types of ants cut up leaves.

appear (appearing, appeared)
1 to look or to seem
She appears to be better today.

2 to come into sight
My sister appeared from behind me.

applause (applauded)
clapping by a group of people to
show they enjoyed something
Everyone applauded at the end.

apple (apples)
a fruit that grows
on trees
*I always have an
apple after lunch.*

apple

apricot (apricots)
a small, fuzzy-skinned
yellow fruit
I like dried apricots on cereal.

apron (aprons)
a piece of cloth that you put over
your clothes to keep them clean
I wore an apron while I was painting.

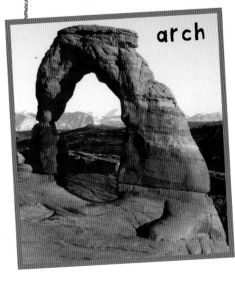
arch

**arch
(arches)**
a curved
structure
*We sat on
the grass
under the
arch.*

a
b
c
d
e
f
g
h
i
j
k
l
m
n
o
p
q
r
s
t
u
v
w
x
y
z

a b c d e f g h i j k l m n o p q r s t u v w x y z

arena (arenas)
a large building where you can
see sports events or concerts
I saw a football match in an arena.

argue (arguing, argued)
to strongly disagree
Let's not argue about the meal.

arm (arms)
the part of your body between
your shoulder and hand
Dad has broken his right arm.

**armchair
(armchairs)**
a chair that has
places for you to
rest your arms
*I like to read when
I'm sitting in an armchair.*

armchair

army (armies)
the people that fight for a
country on land
The Roman army was very powerful.

arrest (arresting, arrested)
to take someone to a police
station because they have
committed a crime
The police arrested the thief.

arrow (arrows)
a pointed stick that you shoot
from a bow
We fired arrows at the enemy.

art
the making of paintings,
drawings and sculpture
My favourite subject at school is art.

artist (artists)
a person who makes art
He is a well-known artist.

ask (asking, asked)
1 to say something to someone
because you want them to tell
you something
"What is the time?" she asked.
2 to say you want something
I asked for a glass of water.

asleep
sleeping
*The baby is
fast asleep.*

asleep

assembly (assemblies)
a meeting of the whole school
We have an assembly every morning in the hall.

astronaut (astronauts)
a person who travels into space in a spacecraft
Astronauts walked on the Moon.

athlete (athletes)
a person who plays a sport
Athletes must train every day.

atlas (atlases)
a book with maps in
I use an atlas at school.

attack (attacking, attacked)
to be violent and fight someone or something
Pirates attacked the ship.

aunt (auntie; aunts, aunties)
the sister of your mother or father, the wife of your uncle
My aunt looks like my mother.

author (authors)
a person who writes books
Philippa Pearce is the author of Tom's Midnight Garden.

autograph (autographs)
the name of a famous person, written by them
Can I have your autograph?

automatic
if a machine is automatic it works by itself
The washing machine is automatic.

astronaut

autumn
the time of year between the summer and the winter
The leaves turn red in autumn.

awake
not sleeping, not asleep
I tried to stay awake all night.

awful
very bad
This medicine tastes awful.

axe (axes)
a tool with a handle and a sharp cutting edge that is used for chopping wood
Dad chopped the tree down with an axe.

axe

a b c d e f g h i j k l m n o p q r s t u v w x y z

a
b
c
d
e
f
g
h
i
j
k
l
m
n
o
p
q
r
s
t
u
v
w
x
y
z

How many things can you spot beginning with 'b'?

Bb

baboon (baboons)
a large monkey
Baboons are very noisy.

baby (babies)
a young child that has not yet learnt to talk or walk
There is a new baby in the family.

baboon

babysitter (babysitters)
a person who looks after children while their parents are out
Our babysitter plays games with us.

back (backs)
1 the part of your body behind you, between your shoulders and bottom
I can swim on my back.

2 the part of something that is furthest from the front or from the way it is facing
The wires are at the back of the computer.

backwards
the direction opposite to the way something is facing
Take four steps backwards.

bacon
meat from a pig
We have bacon and eggs for breakfast.

bad (worse, worst)
not good or pleasant
It's bad news.

badge (badges)
something that you put on your clothes to show who you are or what you have done
I have four swimming badges.

badger (badgers)
an animal with black-and-white fur that lives underground
There is a family of badgers living in the wood.

badly
not done well
I play the piano badly.

badminton
a game that is played with rackets and a small object called a shuttlecock
We play badminton every day.

bag (bags)
a container made of plastic, paper, cloth or leather
Let's put the vegetables into this bag.

baggy (baggier, baggiest)
loose, not tight
My jumper is too big and baggy.

bake (baking, baked)
to cook food in an oven
Bake the cake for 40 minutes.

balance
the ability to stay still without falling over
If I close my eyes I lose my balance.

balance (balancing, balanced)
1 to hold yourself still without falling over
Can you balance on this narrow bar?
2 to keep something steady without dropping it
The seal balanced a ball on its nose.

badminton

a b c d e f g h i j k l m n o p q r s t u v w x y z

a
b
c
d
e
f
g
h
i
j
k
l
m
n
o
p
q
r
s
t
u
v
w
x
y
z

balcony (balconies)
an area outside a window where you can sit or stand
You can see the beach from the balcony.

bald
without hair
My dad is going bald.

bald

ball (balls)
a round object that you throw, hit or kick in games
The ball went into the net.

ballet
a type of dancing that tells a story with no words
A very famous ballet is Swan Lake.

balloon (balloons)
a thin, rubber bag filled with air that is used as a decoration
We had balloons at the party.

balloons

banana (bananas)
a long, curved yellow fruit
I like bananas for breakfast.

band (bands)
1 a thin strip of material
Megan has got a band in her hair.
2 a group of people who play music together
My brother plays the drums in a band.

bandage (bandages)
a piece of material that you wrap around an injury
The nurse put a bandage on Matthew's leg when he fell over.

bang (bangs)
a sudden loud noise
The door shut with a bang.

bank (banks)
1 a place to keep money
There is a bank in the town.
2 the land alongside a river
People sit on the bank and catch fish.

barbecue (barbecues)
a meal cooked over a flame outside
The weather's good. Let's have a barbecue.

bark

the hard material on a tree trunk

The bark is peeling off the tree in some places.

bark (barking, barked)

to make a short, loud noise, like a dog

My dog barks when someone knocks at the door.

barn (barns)

a farm building for keeping animals or crops

The cows are in the barn.

basket (baskets)

a container made of thin strips, to hold or carry things

Put the bread in the basket.

basketball

a game played by two teams that score points by throwing a ball through a round net

Basketball is a fast game.

bat (bats)

1 a small animal that usually flies at night

Bats have big ears and good hearing.

2 the wooden stick used to hit a ball in games such as rounders

I got a cricket bat for my birthday.

bath (baths)

a long container that you fill with water and sit in to wash your body

In our bathroom there's a bath, washbasin and toilet.

battery (batteries)

an object that makes electricity

My torch needs two batteries.

beach (beaches)

the area of land that is next to the sea

We built a sandcastle on the beach.

bean (beans)

the seed of a climbing plant that is eaten as food

I like baked beans on toast.

beans

a b c d e f g h i j k l m n o p q r s t u v w x y z

a
b
c
d
e
f
g
h
i
j
k
l
m
n
o
p
q
r
s
t
u
v
w
x
y
z

bear (bears)
a large, strong wild animal that is covered in fur
Bears sleep all winter.

beard (beards)
hair that grows on a man's chin and cheeks
My Dad has a beard.

beard

beautiful
lovely to look at
Roses are beautiful flowers.

bed (beds)
a piece of furniture for sleeping on
There are two beds in my room.

bedroom (bedrooms)
the room where you sleep
My bedroom is next to the bathroom.

bee (bees)
an insect with yellow-and-black stripes
Bees make honey.

beef
meat from a cow
We had roast beef for dinner.

begin (beginning, began, begun)
to start
The story begins in the forest.

behind
at the back of someone or something
She's hiding behind the garden fence.

bell (bells)
a metal object that makes a ringing sound
The church bells ring every Sunday.

below
in a lower place than something else
The gym is on the floor below.

belt (belts)
a piece of clothing that you wear around your waist
My belt holds my trousers up.

Puzzle time
Untangle the bees to see which one gets home

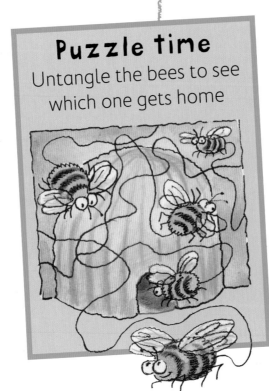

bench (benches)
a long seat for two or more people to sit on
I'll sit on the bench and wait for you.

berry (berries)
a small, soft fruit that grows on bushes or trees
Blackberries and raspberries are types of berries.

better (best)
of a higher standard or quality
The new game is better than the last one.

between
in a place or time that separates two things or people
You can sit between us.

bicycle (bike; bicycles, bikes)
a machine with two wheels that you sit on and move by pushing on pedals
I'd like a new bicycle for my birthday.

bicycle

big (bigger, biggest)
1 large in size, not small
I need a big bag to carry all these books.
2 important
There's a big match today.

bird

bird (birds)
a creature that has wings, feathers, and lays eggs
There's a bird in the tree.

birthday (birthdays)
the day of the year on which a person is born
My birthday is 25 September.

biscuit (biscuits)
a dry, thin cake that is usually sweet
My Mum likes a biscuit with a cup of tea.

bite (biting, bit, bitten)
to cut into something with your teeth
Be careful of the dog. He bites!

a b c d e f g h i j k l m n o p q r s t u v w x y z

a
b
c
d
e
f
g
h
i
j
k
l
m
n
o
p
q
r
s
t
u
v
w
x
y
z

bitter
having a strong, sharp taste such
as coffee
Dark chocolate sometimes tastes
very bitter.

blanket (blankets)
a piece of material on a bed that
you use to keep warm
I'd like an extra blanket on my bed.

blind
not able to see
Some blind people carry
white sticks.

blister (blisters)
a raised piece of
skin, filled with
liquid, caused by
burning or rubbing
I have a blister on my foot.

blizzard (blizzards)
a very heavy snow storm
People shouldn't drive in a blizzard.

blood
red liquid that the heart pumps
through your body
I cut my finger and now there's
blood on my shirt.

blouse (blouses)
a shirt that girls and women
wear
Our school blouse is blue and white.

blow (blowing, blew, blown)
to push air out of your mouth
It's fun to blow bubbles!

boat (boats)
a small ship
You get to the island by boat.

body (bodies)
1 the whole of a
person
Skin covers your
body.
2 a dead person
They covered the
body with a sheet.

boat

bone (bones)
a hard, white part under the skin
of a person or animal
Your skeleton has more than 200
bones.

bonfire (bonfires)
a fire outside
Dad made a bonfire in the garden.

book (books)
1 sheets of paper with writing on, joined together for reading
This is a book about spiders.
2 sheets of paper joined together for writing on
Write your name on the cover of your exercise book.

books

boot (boots)
1 a strong shoe that covers your foot and ankle
Wear your boots in the rain.
2 the part of a car for carrying things
The bags are in the boot.

bored
not interested
I'm bored, let's play a game.

boring
not interesting
This programme's boring. Let's turn the television off.

born
starting life
My Dad was born in 1980.

borrow (borrowing, borrowed)
to take something that belongs to another person and give it back to them later
You can borrow the books for two weeks.

bottle (bottles)
a tall container for storing liquid
I have a water bottle on my bike.

bottom (bottoms)
1 the part of your body that you sit on
I fell on my bottom.
2 the lowest part of something
The number is at the bottom of the page.

bounce (bouncing, bounced)
to move back quickly after hitting or falling on something
The children bounced up and down on the trampoline.

bow (rhymes with low; bows)
1 a knot with loops
I tied my shoelaces in a bow.
2 a long, thin stick with string for shooting arrows or playing an instrument
You play the violin with a bow.

a
b
c
d
e
f
g
h
i
j
k
l
m
n
o
p
q
r
s
t
u
v
w
x
y
z

a
b
c
d
e
f
g
h
i
j
k
l
m
n
o
p
q
r
s
t
u
v
w
x
y
z

bow (rhymes with cow; bowing, bowed)
to bend your body or your head to show respect
The servants all bowed to the king.

bowl (bowls)
a deep, curved dish
You eat cereal out of a bowl.

box (boxes)
a container with four sides
I keep my crayons in a box.

boxing
the sport of fighting with closed hands
My Dad likes watching boxing on TV.

boy (boys)
a male child or a young man
There are two boys in their family.

bracelet (bracelets)
a piece of jewellery worn around the wrist
My bracelet has my name on it.

boy

brain (brains)
the part of your body inside your head that you use for thinking, feeling and moving
When you touch something hot, nerves send a message to your brain and you pull your hand away

branch

branch (branches)
the part of a tree that grows out from the trunk
Leaves, flowers and fruit grow on branches.

brave
not afraid to do dangerous things
Soldiers are very brave.

bread
a type of food made with flour, water and yeast
I like jam on bread.

break (breaking, broke, broken)
to make something separate into two or more pieces
I dropped the glass and broke it.

breakfast (breakfasts)
the first meal of the day
We always have cereal for breakfast.

breath (breaths)
the air that goes in and out of your body
Take a deep breath and smell the fresh air.

breathe (breathing, breathed)
to take air into your body and let it out
Breathe in, and slowly breathe out.

breeze (breezes)
a light wind
There's a lovely warm breeze blowing.

brick (bricks)
a block of baked clay used for building
The wall is made with bricks.

bridge (bridges)
a structure built to join two things
There is a bridge over the river.

bright
1 full of light
It's a bright, sunny day.
2 strong and easy to see
Yellow and orange are bright colours.
3 clever, intelligent
That's a bright idea.

brilliant
1 very bright and strong
There was a brilliant light in the sky.
2 very good at doing something
She's a brilliant scientist.
3 very good or enjoyable
This is a brilliant book, you should read it.

bring (bringing, brought)
to take something with you
Don't forget to bring a packed lunch for the trip.

broccoli
a green vegetable that looks like a little tree
Let's have broccoli with our dinner.

bridge

a b c d e f g h i j k l m n o p q r s t u v w x y z

a
b
c
d
e
f
g
h
i
j
k
l
m
n
o
p
q
r
s
t
u
v
w
x
y
z

broom (brooms)
a brush with a handle
Sweep the floor with a broom.

brother (brothers)
a boy or a man who has the same parents as another person
Nadia has two brothers.

bruise (bruises)
a blue or purple mark on the skin that appears after something has hit you
I've got a big bruise on my arm.

brush (brushes)
a tool that has stiff hairs fastened to a handle that is used for sweeping, painting or cleaning
When you've finished painting, put the brush in the jar of water.

bubble (bubbles)
a small ball of air in a liquid
Lemonade has got lots of little bubbles in it.

bucket (buckets)
a round, open container with a handle
The bucket was full of water.

budgie (budgerigar; budgies, budgerigars)
a small, brightly coloured bird that some people keep as a pet
Our budgie lives in a cage.

budgie

build (building, built)
to make something, such as a house, by putting pieces together
There are plans to build a new school next year.

building (buildings)
a place with a roof and walls
Houses, shops and schools are all buildings.

bull (bulls)
a male cow, elephant or whale
We saw a bull with a ring in his nose.

Puzzle time
Which of these brushes is the odd one out?

Answer: broom, it doesn't end in 'brush'.

bunch (bunches)
a group of things that are attached together
There's a bunch of grapes in my lunchbox.

bunch

burger (burgers)
a flat cake of meat or vegetables
We had burgers and chips for dinner.

burglar (burglars)
a person who goes into buildings to steal things
A burglar stole the money.

burn (burning, burnt, burned)
1 to be on fire
The candles are burning.
2 to destroy something with fire
We burnt all the rubbish on a bonfire.

bus (buses)
a vehicle that carries passengers
I get the bus to school.

bush (bushes)
a small tree with lots of branches
Berries grow on bushes.

busy (busier, busiest)
1 doing things, working hard
Mum's busy on the computer.
2 lively, full of people
The town centre is always very busy on a Saturday.

butcher (butchers)
a person who cuts up and sells meat
Our butcher always wears a striped apron.

butter
yellow food that is made from milk
Use a knife to spread butter on the bread.

butterfly (butterflies)
an insect with large wings
Butterflies drink from flowers.

button (buttons)
a round object that fastens clothes
My shirt has six buttons.

buy (buying, bought)
to get something by paying money for it
Shall we buy some sweets?

a b c d e f g h i j k l m n o p q r s t u v w x y z

a b **c** d e f g h i j k l m n o p q r s t u v w x y z

How many things can you spot beginning with 'c'?

Cc

cabbage (cabbages)
a large vegetable with thick, round leaves
Rabbits love eating cabbages.

cabbage

cabin (cabins)
1 a small house made of wood, usually in the country
The cabin is halfway up the mountain.

2 the place where the passengers sit inside an aeroplane
The pilot walked back through the cabin.

3 a small room to sleep in on a ship
The cabin has two beds.

cactus (cacti or cactuses)
a plant that grows in hot, dry places, and that has needles instead of leaves
Cacti don't need much water.

café (cafés)
a place that serves drinks and simple meals
Why don't we stop and have lunch at a café?

cage (cages)
a room or box with bars in which to keep animals or birds
Pet hamsters and mice live in cages.

cake (cakes)
a sweet food made of flour, sugar and eggs that is baked in an oven
Mum baked me a chocolate cake for my birthday.

calculator (calculators)
a machine that adds up numbers and does other sums
I use a calculator in maths lessons.

calculator

calendar (calendars)
a chart that shows the days, weeks and months of the year
We wrote everyone's birthday on the calendar.

calf (calves)
1 a baby cow, elephant or whale
The calf is two days old.
2 the back part of your leg between your ankle and knee
I've pulled a muscle in my calf.

call (calling, called)
1 to shout or say something in a loud voice
Dad called out to us.
2 to telephone
I'll call you when I get home.
3 to visit
The doctor calls when someone is very ill.
4 to give someone or something a name
They called the baby Luke.

camel (camels)
a large animal with one or two humps that can carry heavy loads
A camel can go without water for a long time.

camel

camera (cameras)
a piece of equipment used for taking photographs or filming
The teacher brought her camera on the school trip.

camp (camps)
a place where people stay in tents
The camp is over the hill.

a b c d e f g h i j k l m n o p q r s t u v w x y z

a b **c** d e f g h i j k l m n o p q r s t u v w x y z

camp (camping, camped)
to stay in a tent
Every summer the Scouts camp in this field.

can (cans)
a metal container
We collect drink cans for charity.

can (could)
1 to be able to do something
Aziz can play the violin.
2 to be allowed to do something
We can come to your party.

candle (candles)
a stick of wax with a string through it that you burn for light
Let's light the candles on the cake.

candles

canoe (canoes)
a small boat which is pointed at both ends
You use a paddle to make a canoe move through the water.

capital (capitals)
the main town in a country
Paris is the capital of France.

capital letter (capital letters)
a large letter of the alphabet
THIS SENTENCE IS WRITTEN IN CAPITAL LETTERS.

captain (captains)
1 someone who leads a team
Who is captain of the football team this year?
2 a person who is in charge of a ship or a plane
The captain has told us the flight will take two hours.

car (cars)
a machine on wheels that has an engine and that people can ride in
There is a car in the driveway.

car

caravan (caravans)
a small house on wheels that can be pulled behind a car
Jack and Katie have taken their caravan on holiday.

card (cards)
1 thick, stiff paper (no plural)
We stuck the pictures onto card.
2 a piece of card with words and a picture that you give or send someone
My brother gave me a birthday card.
3 a piece of stiff paper or plastic that you use to buy things or to identify yourself
I have a library card.
4 a piece of stiff paper with pictures and numbers that you use to play games
Each player has seven cards.

cards

cardigan (cardigans)
a piece of clothing like a jumper with buttons down the front
Wear a cardigan if it's cold.

careful
paying attention to what you are doing so that you don't make a mistake or have an accident
Be careful! That knife is sharp.

caretaker (caretakers)
a person who looks after a building
The caretaker locks up the school at night.

carnival (carnivals)
a big party in the street with music and dancing
People often wear fancy dress at a carnival.

carol (carols)
a religious Christmas song
My favourite carol is Silent Night.

carrots

carpet (carpets)
a thick cover for the floor
The carpet in my bedroom is blue.

carrot (carrots)
a long, orange vegetable that grows under the ground
Carrots are a healthy food to eat.

carry (carrying, carried)
to move something from one place to another
Can you help me carry these bags?

cartoon (cartoons)
1 a funny drawing in a newspaper or comic
There is a cartoon every day in most newspapers.
2 a film with drawings instead of real actors
I like watching cartoons on television.

castle (castles)
a large, strong building with thick walls
Sleeping Beauty lived in a castle.

cat (cats)
a small, furry animal with a long tail and sharp claws
My cat likes to climb trees.

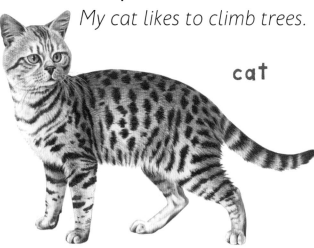

cat

catch (catching, caught)
1 to get hold of something when someone throws it
I'll throw the ball and you can try to catch it.

2 to get an illness
People often catch cold in winter.
3 to get on a bus, train or plane and go somewhere
We usually catch the bus to school.

castle

caterpillar (caterpillars)
an animal, like a worm with legs, that turns into a butterfly or a moth
Caterpillars eat leaves.

cave (caves)
a hole in a mountainside or under the ground
Caves are usually dark and damp.

CD (compact disc; CDs, compact discs)
a circular piece of plastic for storing sound
Have you bought their latest CD? It's really good!

celery
a long, green, crunchy vegetable
Mum chopped up some celery.

cellar (cellars)
a room underneath a house or
other building
We keep our bikes in the cellar.

cello (cellos)
a large musical instrument that
you sit down to play
Cellos look like big violins.

cereal
a breakfast food that is made
from wheat, oats or rice
I always put sugar on my cereal.

chair (chairs)
a piece of furniture for sitting on
Pull your chair close to the desk.

chalk
a soft, white rock
I drew a picture using chalk.

**chameleon
(chameleons)**
a lizard that
changes
colour so its
skin matches the
things around it
*A chameleon catches its prey
using its long, sticky tongue.*

chameleon

change (changing, changed)
1 to become different or to make
something different
You haven't changed at all!
2 to put on different clothes
I'm cold – I'll change my top.

cheap
not expensive
*My watch was cheap. I bought
it in the sale.*

cheese
a food
that is made
from milk
Can I have cheese on toast for tea?

cheese

cheetah (cheetahs)
a wild animal of the cat family
with black spots
Cheetahs can run very fast.

cherry (cherries)
a small, round, reddish fruit
with a stone in the centre
*We had cherries and ice
cream for dessert.*

chess
a board game for two people
Chess is my favourite game.

a b c d e f g h i j k l m n o p q r s t u v w x y z

chimpanzees

chest (chests)
1 the part of your body between your neck and your stomach
Men have hair on their chests.
2 a strong box with a top that locks
The pirates hid the gold in a chest.

chestnut (chestnuts)
a big, brown, shiny nut which grows on trees
We had roasted chestnuts at the party.

chicken (chickens)
a farm bird kept for its eggs and meat, or the meat from this bird
A female chicken is called a hen.

child (children)
1 a young person
Every child has to go to school
2 someone's son or daughter
My eldest sister has just one child.

chimney (chimneys)
an opening over a fire that takes smoke out through the roof of a building
Smoke was coming from the chimney.

chimpanzee (chimp; chimpanzees, chimps)
a small ape with fur and no tail
Chimpanzees are closely related to humans.

chin (chins)
the part of your face under your mouth
His beard hides his chin.

chips
pieces of potato fried in oil
Do you like fish and chips?

chocolate
a sweet food made from cocoa beans
Would you like a piece of chocolate?

chocolate

choir (choirs)
a group of singers
I sing in the school choir.

Christmas
a Christian holiday in December
I got lots of presents for Christmas.

church (churches)
the place where Christians meet
to worship
My uncle got married in a church.

cinema (cinemas)
a place you go to see films
Shall we go to the cinema?

circus (circuses)
a show with people
and animals, held
in a big tent
The circus is in town!

city (cities)
a large town
London is the biggest city in Britain.

clap (clapping, clapped)
to make a loud sound by hitting
the palms of your hands together
We clapped at the end of the show.

class (classes)
1 a group of people who learn
together
We're in the same class.

claws

2 a group of things or animals
that are similar
*People belong to the class of
animals called mammals.*

classroom (classrooms)
a room in a school where you
have lessons
Our classroom is next to the hall.

claw (claws)
a sharp, hard nail on an animal's
foot
My cat scratched me with her claws.

clean
not dirty
The car is clean and shiny.

clean (cleaning, cleaned)
to make something tidy, to
take dirt away
*Mum told me to clean my room
because it was very messy.*

clear
1 easy to understand, hear or
read
The instructions are clear.
2 easy to see through
*You can see the fish swimming in
the clear water.*

a b **c** d e f g h i j k l m n o p q r s t u v w x y z

a
b
c
d
e
f
g
h
i
j
k
l
m
n
o
p
q
r
s
t
u
v
w
x
y
z

clever
able to learn or understand things quickly or well
Well done. You're very clever.

cliff (cliffs)
a rock or mountain next to the sea
The road runs along a cliff.

climb (climbing, climbed)
to move upwards
She climbed to the top of the ladder.

cloakroom (cloakrooms)
a room where you hang your coat
We each have our own peg in the cloakroom.

clock (clocks)
a machine that tells the time
The clock said 5:55 a.m.

close (rhymes with dose)
near
The hotel is close to the beach.

close (closing, closed) (rhymes with rose)
to shut
The shops close at six o'clock.

clock

cloth (cloths)
1 a soft material
The chair is covered in cloth.
2 a piece of cloth for a special purpose
Clean the window with a cloth.

clothes
things that people wear
I've grown and now my clothes don't fit me.

cloud (clouds)
a white or grey object in the sky that is made of tiny drops of water
There are a few clouds in the sky.

clown (clowns)
someone who makes people laugh
There was a clown at Tom's party.

coach (coaches)
1 a large bus
We went to the zoo by coach.
2 a person who trains people in sport
The football team is looking for a new coach.

coast

the land next to the sea
The village is on the coast.

coat (coats)

a piece of clothing you wear over your clothes to stay warm
I hang my coat on my peg when I get to school.

cobweb

cobweb (cobwebs)

a thin net that a spider spins to catch insects
There are cobwebs in the cellar.

coconut (coconuts)

the nut of the palm tree
Coconuts have a white juice inside them.

cocoon (cocoons)

the bag around an insect that protects it while it is growing into an adult
The cocoon broke open and a butterfly flew out.

coffee

a hot drink made from the brown beans of a plant
Do you take sugar in your coffee?

coin (coins)

a piece of money that is made of metal
They keep coins from their holidays.

cold

not warm or hot
Brrr – this water is very cold.

collect (collecting, collected)

to put things together in one place
Some people collect stamps.

colour (colours)

blue, green, red or yellow
What colour is your jacket?

colour (colouring, coloured)

to make something a colour, for example with paint or crayons
We coloured the picture in.

comb

comb (combs)

an object for making your hair tidy
Don't let anyone use your comb.

comic (comics)

a magazine with pictures that tell a story
The story in this comic is very funny.

a
b
c
d
e
f
g
h
i
j
k
l
m
n
o
p
q
r
s
t
u
v
w
x
y
z

compass (compasses)
an object that shows you what direction you are travelling in
Read the compass to find the treasure!

competition (competitions)
a test to see who is best at something
There was a singing competition on the radio.

complain (complaining, complained)
to say that something is wrong and that you are unhappy with it
He complained to the waiter.

computer (computers)
a machine for storing information and doing jobs such as writing letters
You can play games on computers.

concentrate (concentrating, concentrated)
to pay attention to what you are doing
I can't concentrate on my work because it's so noisy.

cook

concert (concerts)
a show where people play music
I'm playing the violin in the concert tonight.

confused
a feeling of not being sure
I was confused by the question.

container (containers)
something that holds something else in it
Jars, tins and boxes are containers.

continent (continents)
one of the seven large areas of land in the world
Asia, Africa and Europe are all continents.

cook (cooks)
a person who prepares food
The cook has to make meals for 200 children every day.

cook (cooking, cooked)
to make food hot so it can be eaten
Ahmed is cooking dinner for us.

cool
a little bit cold
There is a cool breeze.

copy (copying, copied)
to do something the same as something else
The teacher writes a sentence and we copy it.

corn
the seeds of plants such as wheat and oats
Popcorn and cornflakes are made from corn.

cottage

cottage (cottages)
a small house, usually in the country
My granny lives in a little cottage.

cough (coughing, coughed)
to force air from your throat
She's still coughing. Give her a drink of water.

count (counting, counted)
to find out how many
The teacher counted the books.

country (countries)
1 a place with its own government
France and Italy are European countries.
2 land away from cities and towns
We live in a village in the country.

cousin (cousins)
the child of your aunt or uncle
Charlie is my cousin.

cow (cows, cattle)
a large, female farm animal that gives milk
Cows eat grass.

cowboy (cowboys)
a man who rides a horse and takes care of cattle
The cowboy is wearing a big hat and boots.

crab (crabs)
a sea creature that moves sideways and has big claws
I saw a crab in a pool on the beach.

crab

a b c d e f g h i j k l m n o p q r s t u v w x y z

crack (cracks)
a line where something
is broken
There's a crack in this mug.

**crack (cracking,
cracked)**
to break something so
that a line appears on it
I've cracked this mug. Sorry!

crane (cranes)
a large machine that lifts very
heavy things
*The crane lifted the huge box and
put it on the ship.*

crash (crashes)
1 an accident when two or more
things bump into each other
My uncle had a crash in his car.
2 a loud noise
The loud crash hurt my ears.

crash (crashing, crashed)
1 to have an accident by
bumping into something
*The car crashed into a
tree.*
2 to suddenly stop working
*The computer has crashed and
now I've lost all my work.*

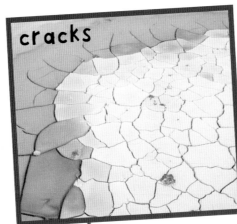

cracks

**crawl (crawling,
crawled)**
to move around
on your hands
and knees
*The baby is
starting to crawl.*

crayon (crayons)
a small pencil made from
coloured wax
Use crayons to finish the picture.

cream
1 the thick yellowish-white liquid
at the top of milk
*I love strawberries and cream in
summer.*
2 a thick substance that you rub
in your skin
Don't forget to put sun cream on.

creature (creatures)
any animal
The blue whale is a huge creature.

crash

creep (creeping, crept)
to move so that no one sees or
hears you
We crept quietly through the bushes.

cricket
1 a game played by two teams.
The aim is to hit the ball and
score runs
*At my school we play football in
winter and cricket in summer.*
2 (crickets) an insect which
makes a noise by rubbing its
wings together
Crickets live under rocks and logs.

crisps
fried, thin slices of potato
I love eating crisps.

crocodile

crocodile (crocodiles)
a large animal with a long body,
short legs and big teeth
Crocodiles like floating in the water.

crooked
not straight
The fence is very crooked.

crop (crops)
plants that are grown for people
and animals to eat, or that are
used to make things
*The weather is very important to
farmers who grow crops.*

cross (crosses)
two lines that go over each other
like the letter x
*There is a cross on the map where
the treasure is hidden.*

cross (crossing, crossed)
to go from one side of something
to the other
*We looked both ways then crossed
the road.*

crowd (crowds)
a lot of people in one place
*There was a big crowd of
people outside the shop.*

crown

crown (crowns)
a metal circle that kings
and queens wear on their heads
The king is wearing a gold crown.

cruel (crueller, cruellest)
not kind
We must not be cruel to animals.

a b c d e f g h i j k l m n o p q r s t u v w x y z

crumb (crumbs)
a small piece of something such as bread or cake
Who's eaten the cake? There are only a few crumbs left.

cry (crying, cried)
1 to have tears coming from your eyes, usually because you feel sad or are hurt
The little boy cried when he fell over.
2 to shout
"Help! Help!" they cried.

crying

cucumber (cucumbers)
a long, thin green vegetable that you put in salads
Cucumbers contain a lot of water.

cuddle (cuddling, cuddled)
to hold someone in your arms to show you care
Chloe cuddled her friend to cheer her up.

cup (cups)
a container with a handle for drinking from
I'd like a cup of hot milk please.

cupboard (cupboards)
a piece of furniture for storing things
Please dry the dishes and put them in the cupboard.

curious
wanting to know or find out about something
Cats are very curious.

curls

curl (curls)
a piece of hair that is curved at the end
She has beautiful curls.

curtain (curtains)
cloth that hangs across or over a window
We close the curtains at night.

cushion (cushions)
a bag with soft material inside for sitting or lying on
This chair is hard. I'm going to put a cushion on it.

cut (cutting, cut)
to use a knife or scissors to break something or make it smaller
We all sang 'Happy Birthday', then she cut the cake.

a b c d e f g h i j k l m n o p q r s t u v w x y z

How many things can you spot beginning with 'd'?

D d

damage (damaging, damaged)
to spoil or break something
A big dog damaged the garden fence.

dance (dancing, danced)
to move your body to music
Let's dance to this music.

daffodil (daffodils)
a yellow flower
that comes out
in spring
*I bought my mum a
bunch of daffodils.*

daffodils

**dandelion
(dandelions)**
a wild flower with
thin, yellow petals
and fluffy seeds
*There are dandelions
growing on the lawn.*

daisy (daisies)
a flower with white
petals and a yellow centre
*Sophie picked some daisies to make
a daisy chain.*

dangerous
not safe
Playing with matches is dangerous.

a b c **d** e f g h i j k l m n o p q r s t u v w x y z

abcdefghijklmnopqrstuvwxyz

dark
not light
It's too dark to play outside.

date (dates)
1 the number of a day in a month
What's the date today?
2 a sweet fruit from a palm tree
Dates are sticky and chewy.

daughter (daughters)
a female child
Mr and Mrs Patel have two daughters.

day (days)
1 a 24-hour period
We're staying here for three days.
2 the time between the early morning when the sun rises and the time it sets
Bats do not fly during the day.

dead
not alive
This plant looks dead. Did you water it?

deaf
not able to hear
Many deaf people can read lips.

dear
1 a word to start a letter
Dear Aran, How are you?
2 much loved
She's a very dear friend.
3 expensive
This dress is too dear, let's find a cheaper one.

deep
a long way from the top to the bottom
I'm not afraid to swim in the deep end of the pool.

deer

deer
an animal that lives in forests
Deer are gentle animals.

delicious
tasting very good
This ice cream is delicious.

delighted
very happy
I'm delighted with my new bike.

den (dens)

1 a wild animal's home

The fox went back to its den.

2 a structure that children play or hide in

We made a den out of cardboard boxes.

dentist (dentists)

a person who looks after people's teeth

I go to the dentist every six months.

desert (deserts)

a place where there is very little or no rain

Camels live in the desert.

desk (desks)

a piece of furniture that you sit at to read, write or use a computer

There's a lamp on my desk.

dessert (desserts)

sweet food that you eat at the end of a meal

What's for dessert? Is it ice cream?

dessert

detective (detectives)

a person who follows clues to find out about a crime and who did it

The detective asked everyone questions.

diamond (diamonds)

a very hard, clear stone which is used to make jewellery

Diamonds are very expensive.

diary (diaries)

a book with the days of the year in it where you write what you plan to do, or what you have done

I write in my diary before I go to bed each night.

dice

die (dice)

a cube with spots on each side that is used for playing games

It's your turn – throw the dice.

die (dying, died)

to stop living

Water the plant before it dies.

a b c **d** e f g h i j k l m n o p q r s t u v w x y z

different
not the same
The two sisters are very different.

difficult
not easy
I hope the spelling test isn't too difficult.

dig (digging, dug)
to make a hole in the ground
Let's dig a hole in the sand.

digital
1 showing information using numbers that can change
This is a digital watch.
2 storing information using a special computer code
My mum uses a digital camera.

dining room (dining rooms)
the room in which you eat your meals
The dining room is next to the kitchen in our house.

dinner (dinners)
the main evening meal
We're having lasagne and salad for dinner.

dinner

dinosaur (dinosaurs)
an animal that became extinct millions of years ago
We learnt all about dinosaurs at the history museum.

dinosaur

dirty (dirtier, dirtiest)
not clean
Please take your dirty shoes off before you come in.

disabled
a disabled person cannot use part of their body
This parking space is for disabled drivers only.

disappear (disappearing, disappeared)
to go out of sight or become impossible to find
The sun disappeared behind a cloud.

disco (discos)
a place or a party where people dance
There's a disco on Saturday.

discover (discovering, discovered)
to find something for the first time
The farmer discovered some old coins in his field.

disease (diseases)
an illness
Injections stop you from getting some diseases.

disguise (disguises)
something that you wear to hide who you really are
He came to the party in disguise.

dish (dishes)
a bowl or plate, used for serving food
Please dry the dishes.

disk (disks)
a thin, round piece of plastic for storing computer information
Save the file on a disk.

district (districts)
an area of a town or country
Emily and I live in the same district.

dive

disturb (disturbing, disturbed)
to speak to someone when they are doing something
Please don't disturb James while he's doing his homework.

ditch (ditches)
a long, narrow hole in the ground along the side of a road or field
Don't fall into the ditch!

dive (diving, dived)
to go into water headfirst
I can dive to the bottom of the pool.

divide (dividing, divided)
to separate or share something
Let's divide the pizza between us.

dizzy (dizzier, dizziest)
feeling that things are turning around you or that you are going to fall
That ride makes me dizzy.

doctor (doctors)
a person who looks after sick people
My uncle is a doctor. He works at the hospital.

a b c **d** e f g h i j k l m n o p q r s t u v w x y z

abcdefghijklmnopqrstuvwxyz

document (documents)
1 a set of papers that contain official information
We keep important documents in this cupboard.
2 a piece of work that is saved in a file on a computer
You can attach a document to an email.

dog (dogs)
an animal that people keep as a pet
Our dog is called Prince.

dog

doll (dolls)
a toy in the shape of a person
Let's play with our dolls.

dolphin (dolphins)
a large, warm-blooded creature that lives in the ocean
A dolphin looks like a fish but it is an air-breathing mammal.

domino (dominoes)
a piece of black wood or plastic with white spots that is used to play games
Each person has five dominoes.

donkey (donkeys)
an animal that looks like a small horse with long ears
Every day we feed carrots to the donkey in the field near our house.

door (doors)
something that you open and close to go into or out of a room, house or car
It's cold, shall we shut the door?

doughnut (doughnuts)
a small, round, sugary cake that has been fried in hot oil
Some doughnuts have a hole in the middle.

dolphins

down
towards a lower place
Get down off the ladder.

download (downloading, downloaded)
to put information from the Internet onto your computer or other electronic device
I downloaded the song to my iPod.

dragon

dragon (dragons)
an imaginary animal like a big lizard that breathes fire
The story is about a princess trapped in a dragon's cave.

dramatic
very exciting with lots of action
The programme had a very dramatic ending.

draughts
a board game for two people
In draughts, each player has twelve pieces.

draw (drawing, drew, drawn)
to make a picture
I can't draw people very well.

drawer (drawers)
part of a piece of furniture that slides in and out that is used for storing things
Put the socks in the drawer.

dream (dreams)
a story that happens in your mind when you are asleep
I had a bad dream last night.

dream (dreaming, dreamt, dreamed)
1 to see things in your sleep
I dreamt that I could fly.
2 to hope for something
We dream of winning the World Cup.

dress (dresses)
a piece of clothing for girls or women that has a top and skirt
I'm wearing a dress for the party.

dress

dress (dressing, dressed)
to put clothes on yourself or someone else
My mum dresses us alike because we're twins.

a
b
c
d
e
f
g
h
i
j
k
l
m
n
o
p
q
r
s
t
u
v
w
x
y
z

dressing gown (dressing gowns)

a long, loose garment like a coat that you wear over pyjamas

She opened the door in her dressing gown.

drink (drinks)

liquid that you take in your mouth and swallow

I'm thirsty. Can I have a drink please?

drink (drinking, drank, drunk)

to take liquid into your mouth and swallow it

I drank a glass of water.

drive (driving, drove, driven)

to control a vehicle, such as a car

Our mum drives us to and from school every day.

drop (dropping, dropped)

to fall or to let something fall

Don't drop that vase.

drum (drums)

a musical instrument that you hit with a stick or your hand

My brother got a drum for his birthday.

dry (drier, driest or dryer, dryest)

not wet

The washing is nearly dry.

duck (ducks)

a bird with webbed feet that lives near water

We feed bread to the ducks.

ducks

dustbin (dustbins)

a big container for storing rubbish

The dustbin needs emptying.

duvet (duvets)

a large bag of feathers or other soft material that you put on a bed

I curled up under the duvet.

DVD (digital versatile disk; DVDs)

a circular piece of plastic used for storing and playing music and films

We watched a DVD last night.

How many things can you spot beginning with 'e'?

Ee

eagle (eagles)
a bird that hunts for its food
An eagle has sharp claws called talons.

ear (ears)
one of two parts of your body that you hear with
Amy's hair covers her ears.

early (earlier, earliest)
before the normal time
I wake up early in the summer.

earn (earning, earned)
to get money for work
I earn extra pocket money for washing the car.

earring (earrings)
a piece of jewellery that is worn on the ear
My mum got a pair of earrings for her birthday.

eagles

a b c d **e** f g h i j k l m n o p q r s t u v w x y z

a b c d **e** f g h i j k l m n o p q r s t u v w x y z

Earth (earth)
1 the planet we live on
Earth travels around the Sun.
2 soil
A worm is moving through the earth.

Earth

earthquake (earthquakes)
a strong shaking of the earth
The earthquake did lots of damage.

Easter
a Christian holiday in March or April
We're spending Easter at home.

easy (easier, easiest)
not difficult
This book is easy to read.

eat (eating, ate, eaten)
to take food into your mouth and swallow it
We eat our lunch in the canteen.

echo (echoes)
a sound that bounces off something and can be heard again
Can you hear an echo?

eclipse (eclipses)
a situation where the Moon passes in front of the Sun and hides it for a short time
Next week there will be an eclipse of the Sun.

eel (eels)
a long fish that looks like a snake
Eels swim thousands of miles across the Atlantic Ocean.

egg (eggs)
1 an oval object with a shell that some animals lay, and from which their babies hatch
The hen has just laid an egg.
2 an egg used as food
Fried eggs are definitely my favourite breakfast.

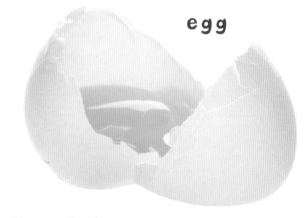

egg

elbow (elbows)
the place where your arm bends
Ouch; I bumped my elbow.

electricity
power that is used to make lights
and machines work
Lightning is a big spark of electricity.

elephant (elephants)
a large, wild animal with a
long nose called a trunk
*There's a new baby
elephant in the zoo.*

elephants

email (emails)
a message sent
by computer
I received emails from all my friends.

email (emailing, emailed)
to send a message by computer
Could you email me the information?

emergency (emergencies)
something very serious that
happens suddenly and which
needs people to take action
immediately
*The guide told us what
to do in an emergency.*

empty
with nothing inside
The box is empty.

end (ends)
the place or time when
something stops
Keep walking to the end of the road.

end (ending, ended)
to finish or stop
*The film ends at
6:30 p.m.*

enemy (enemies)
someone who does not like
you, or wants to hurt you
We are enemies, not friends.

energy
strength or power
*We're trying to save energy, so
we've switched the lights off.*

engine (engines)
1 a machine that makes
something work
*Most cars have their engines at the
front.*

2 the part of a train that
pulls the other carriages
*Thomas is the name of a
fictional tank
engine in a
series of
stories.*

empty

a b c d **e** f g h i j k l m n o p q r s t u v w x y z

enjoy (enjoying, enjoyed)
to like to do something
I enjoy playing tennis.

enormous
very, very big
*Whales are
enormous
creatures.*

enough
as much as you need
There is enough for everyone.

enter (entering, entered)
1 to go into a place
*The children entered the hall and
sat down.*
2 to put information into a
computer
*You need to enter your name and
address on this form.*

entrance (entrances)
the door or way in to a place
The entrance to the cave was dark.

envelope (envelopes)
a paper cover for
letters and cards
*Put a stamp on the
envelope.*

environment
everything around us, such as
land, air or water
*They live in a hot
environment.*

equal

equal
the same as
something else in
number or amount
*One kilogram is equal to
1000 grams.*

equal (equalling, equalled)
to be the same as something else
in number or amount
*One hundred centimetres equal
one metre.*

Equator
an imaginary line round the
centre of the Earth
*Countries near the Equator are very
hot.*

equipment
things that are used to do a
job or activity
*Our school has lots
of new computer
equipment.*

envelopes

error (errors)
a mistake
There are lots of errors in your work.

escalator (escalators)
a staircase that moves
We went up the escalator.

escape (escaping, escaped)
to get away from a place and
be free
A tiger escaped from the zoo.

**estimate (estimating,
estimated)**
to guess the size or cost of
something
We estimated the height of the tree.

evening (evenings)
the time of day between
afternoon and night time
*We don't go to school in
the evening.*

**exaggerate
(exaggerating,
exaggerated)**
to say that something is bigger or
better than it really is
*Don't exaggerate! It didn't cost
that much.*

excellent
very good
*This is an excellent book. I really
like it.*

excited
happy and interested in
something
I am excited about tomorrow.

excursion (excursions)
a trip or an outing
*We're going on an excursion to a
theme park tomorrow.*

excuse (excuses)
a reason you give for something
that you have said or done
*Her excuse for being late is that she
couldn't find her bag.*

exercise

exercise
activity that keeps you
fit and healthy
*Don't watch television.
Go and do some exercise.*

exhibition (exhibitions)
a show where people can look at
things like paintings
*There is an exhibition of things we
made at school.*

a b c d e f g h i j k l m n o p q r s t u v w x y z

a
b
c
d
e
f
g
h
i
j
k
l
m
n
o
p
q
r
s
t
u
v
w
x
y
z

exit (exits)
the way to leave a place
Don't use this door. The exit is over there.

expensive
costing a lot of money
Diamonds are expensive.

experiment (experiments)
a test that you do to learn something or find out if something is true
We did an experiment to see what happens when you put a magnet near a compass.

explain (explaining, explained)
to say what something means or why it has happened
Our teacher explained how the equipment worked.

explanation (explanations)
something that explains what something means or why it happened
There is a good explanation for the accident.

explode (exploding, exploded)
to suddenly burst or blow up into small pieces
The fireworks exploded in the night sky.

explore (exploring, explored)
to look around a new place
We explored the cave.

explosion (explosions)
a loud bang that you hear when something blows up
There was an explosion and then we saw a lot of smoke.

extinct
no longer existing
The dodo is an extinct bird.

extra
more than is necessary
If a lot of people come to the show we'll need some extra chairs.

eye (eyes)
the part of the body that we use to see
I have got blue eyes.

eye

How many things can you spot beginning with 'f'?

a b c d e **f** g h i j k l m n o p q r s t u v w x y z

Ff

face (faces)
the front part of your head
I wash my face every morning.

fact (facts)
something that is true or that really happened
We need to know all the facts.

factory (factories)
a place where things are made in large numbers by machines and people
Dad works at the car factory.

faint
1 not strong or easy to hear, see or smell
I can't see it well because the writing is very faint.
2 feeling weak and dizzy
I feel faint because I'm very hungry.

faint (fainting, fainted)
to suddenly become weak or dizzy and fall down
It was so hot that Sophie fainted.

fair
1 good and reasonable
It's not fair that you've got more sweets than me.
2 light-coloured
He has fair hair.
3 fine, pleasant
The forecast says that the weather will be fair today.

fair

a b c d e **f** g h i j k l m n o p q r s t u v w x y z

fairground (fairgrounds)
a place in the open air with rides and stalls
There are dodgems and a rollercoaster at the fairground.

fairy (fairies)
a person with magic powers in stories
There are good fairies and a bad fairy in Sleeping Beauty.

fairy

fairy tale (fairy tales)
a story for children about magical things
Cinderella *is my favourite fairy tale.*

fake
not real
Her coat is made of fake fur.

fall (falling, fell, fallen)
to drop downwards
The leaves fall from the trees in autumn.

false
not true, correct or real
He gave a false name.

family (families)
a group of people who are related to each other
There are nine people in their family.

famous
very well-known
He's a famous singer.

fan (fans)
1 an object that you hold in your hand and wave, or a machine that moves the air to make it cooler
Sit in front of the fan if you're hot.
2 someone who likes a particular thing or person very much
My dad is a fan of Manchester United.

fancy dress
clothes that you wear to a party to make you look like another person or like an animal
Are you wearing fancy dress to the party?

fang

fang (fangs)
an animal's long, sharp tooth
Wolves and snakes have fangs.

far (farther, farthest; further, furthest)
not near, at a distance away
The station is in the High Street; it's not far.

farm (farms)
a place where people grow crops and keep animals
My uncle's farm has a lot of cows.

fast
quick, not slow
Racing cars are very fast.

fat (fatter, fattest)
1 weighing more than is good or normal
It isn't healthy to be too fat.
2 thick, big or wide
Our teacher reads to us from a big, fat book.

father (fathers)
a male parent, your dad
My father was born in India.

favourite
liked the best
Blue is my favourite colour.

fax (faxes)
1 a machine that sends documents down a telephone line
The secretary sent the document by fax.
2 a document sent by fax
There's a fax for you.

fear (fearing, feared)
to be afraid that something bad is going to happen
Don't worry; there is nothing to fear!

feast (feasts)
a large, special meal to celebrate something
Christmas dinner is a feast at our house.

feather

feather (feathers)
one of the soft, light things that cover a bird's body
The feather floated slowly to the ground.

feed (feeding, fed)
to give food to a person or an animal
It's fun to feed the ducks.

father

feel (feeling, felt)
1 to have an emotion
I feel happy!
2 to touch something
The doctor felt my arm.

female (females)
a woman, girl or animal that can have babies when adult
The farmer separated the females from the males.

fence (fences)
a wall made of wood or wire
There is a fence between our garden and the road.

fence

ferry (ferries)
a type of ship that carries passengers over a short distance
We went to France by ferry.

few
not many, a small number
There are only a few tickets left.

fiction
a story which is made up and not about real people
J K Rowling writes fiction for children.

fidget (fidgeting, fidgeted)
to keep moving and wriggling about
Don't fidget, please. Sit still!

field (fields)
a piece of land for growing crops, raising animals or playing sports
There is a bull in that field.

fierce
angry and strong, or violent
Guard dogs can be very fierce.

fight (fights)
a situation where people try to hurt each other
There was a fight in the car park.

fight (fighting, fought)
when people fight they hit and try to hurt each other
Some people were fighting in the car park.

figure (figures)
1 a written number
Two hundred and fifty-one in figures is 251.
2 a person's shape
She saw the figure of a woman in the shadows.

file (files)
1 a cardboard folder or a box to keep papers in
I keep my postcards in this green file.
2 information on a computer
Move your files to a new folder.

fill (filling, filled)
to put things into something until it is full
Fill the vase with water before putting the flowers in.

film (films)
1 a movie that you watch at the cinema or on the television
There's a Harry Potter film on the television tonight.
2 thin plastic used in some cameras to take photographs
Digital cameras don't use film.

final (finals)
the last match in a competition
Our team is playing in the final.

final
last, happening at the end
You'll find out what happens in the final chapter.

find (finding, found)
to see or get something that you are looking for
I've lost my bag. Can you help me find it?

fine
1 very thin or in small pieces
The beach is covered with fine, white sand.
2 very good
They are fine singers.

finger (fingers)
one of the five long parts on your hand
Some people wear rings on their fingers.

fingers

finish (finishing, finished)
to end
Put your pencil down when you have finished.

fire (fires)
something that burns, giving out heat and flames
We sat around the fire.

fire

a b c d e **f** g h i j k l m n o p q r s t u v w x y z

fire engine (fire engines)
a truck used to put out fires
The fire engine went along the road flashing its lights.

firework (fireworks)
a small object that explodes into bright colours in the sky
We're going to see the fireworks in the park tonight.

fish (plural is the same)
a creature that lives in water
Fish have fins to help them swim, and they breathe through gills.

fist (fists)
a closed hand
Make a fist with your hand.

fish

fit (fitter, fittest)
healthy and strong
I am very fit because I walk a lot.

fit (fitting, fitted)
to be the right size
My shoes don't fit; they're too small.

fix (fixing, fixed)
1 to mend, to repair
The plumber fixed the washing machine.

2 to stick or attach
Fix the picture to the wall.

fizzy (fizzier, fizziest)
having a lot of tiny bubbles
Fizzy drinks aren't very healthy.

flag (flags)
a piece of cloth that is used as a signal, or the sign of a country
The British flag is red, white and blue.

flame (flames)
burning gas from a fire, or bright light from a candle
The candle flames lit up the room.

flash (flashes)
a burst of light
There was a flash of light in the sky.

flash (flashing, flashed)
to shine very brightly, but only for a short time
A light flashed on and off in the distance.

fix

flat (flats)
a room or rooms in a bigger building
My uncle lives in a third-floor flat.

flat (flatter, flattest)
not bumpy or hilly, smooth
The ground is very flat round here.

flavours

flavour (flavours)
the taste of something
*Chocolate and vanilla
are flavours of ice cream.*

Puzzle time
Can you guess these
flavours?
1. v_nilla   2. choc_l_te
3. str_wberr_   4. ban_n_

Answers: 1. vanilla
2. chocolate 3. strawberry
4. banana

flight (flights)
a journey in a plane
Our flight leaves at 9 o'clock.

float (floating, floated)
to lie on the water without
sinking
We floated in the pool.

flood (floods)
a lot of water in a place that is
usually dry
*There were heavy rains and then a
flood.*

floor (floors)
part of a room that you stand on
There was a carpet on the floor.

flour
powder made from wheat which
is used to make bread and cakes
*Mix the flour and
butter together.*

flower (flowers)
the brightly
coloured part of a
plant that makes
the seeds or fruit
*Roses and daffodils
are flowers.*

flu (influenza)
an illness like a very bad cold
*I was off school last week because
I had flu.*

fly (flies)
a small insect with wings
A fly buzzed past me.

fly (flying, flew, flown)
to move through the air
*Some birds fly south in
the winter.*

flying

fog
mist or cloud
*We can't see anything
because of the fog.*

a b c d e **f** g h i j k l m n o p q r s t u v w x y z

a
b
c
d
e
f
g
h
i
j
k
l
m
n
o
p
q
r
s
t
u
v
w
x
y
z

fold (folding, folded)
to turn or bend something over on itself
Fold your clothes before you put them in the drawer.

follow (following, followed)
to move after or behind someone or something
The rats followed the Pied Piper.

follow

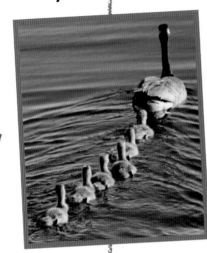

food
something that people or animals eat
This food tastes delicious.

foolish
silly
It is a foolish idea.

foot (feet)
the part of your body at the end of your leg that you stand and walk on
My father has very big feet.

football
a game that is played by two teams who try to kick a ball into a net to score goals
We play football every day.

forest (forests)
a large area of land with lots of trees growing close together
Hansel and Gretel got lost in the forest.

forget (forgetting, forgotten)
to fail to remember something
Don't forget to do your homework.

fork (forks)
1 something with a handle and points that is used for eating or digging
Use your knife and fork.
2 the place where a road or river divides in two
Which way do we go? There's a fork in the road.

forwards
towards the front
Take a step forwards.

fossil (fossils)
the print of an animal or plant that lived long ago
Fossils show us about living things millions of years ago.

fossil

fountain (fountains)
a jet of water that is pushed up
into the air
There is a fountain in the city centre.

fox (foxes)
a wild animal that looks
like a dog with a bushy tail
I saw a fox in the bushes.

fox

fraction (fractions)
a part of something
*One half, one third and
one quarter are fractions.*

frame (frames)
a wood or metal thing that fits
around a door, window or picture
Granny put my photo in a frame.

freckle (freckles)
a small, reddish-brown spot on a
person's skin
I have freckles on my face.

free
1 not controlled, being able to do
what you want
*I have free time on Wednesday
afternoon.*
2 not costing anything
It's free to get in the museum.

freeze (freezing, froze, frozen)
to turn to ice because the
temperature is very cold
Water freezes at 0°C.

fresh
1 just picked, grown or made
*Fresh fruits and vegetables are
healthy foods.*
2 clean and pure
*I'm going outside to get some
fresh air.*

**fridge (fridges; refrigerator,
refrigerators)**
a machine to keep food cool
Put the milk back in the fridge.

friend (friends)
a person you know and like
My friends are coming to my party.

friendly (friendlier, friendliest)
kind and easy to get on with
We have very friendly neighbours.

**frighten (frightening,
frightened)**
to scare, to
make afraid
*Storms may
frighten animals.*

frighten

a b c d e **f** g h i j k l m n o p q r s t u v w x y z

frog (frogs)
a creature, often green, that has long legs and lives on land and in water
There are frogs in the pond.

full

full
containing as much as possible
Is the tank full yet?

fun
an enjoyable activity
We had great fun at the party.

front
the part of something that is the most forward
I sit at the front of the class.

funny (funnier, funniest)
making you laugh
The cartoon is very funny.

frost
white, icy powder that forms when it is very cold outside
The trees are covered in frost.

fur
soft, thick hair on the skin of an animal
The kitten has soft, fluffy fur.

frown (frowning, frowned)
to have a sad, angry or worried look on your face
What's the matter? Why are you frowning?

furniture
things such as chairs, tables, beds and desks
We have some new furniture.

future
the time after now
I wonder what life will be like in the future.

fruit (fruits or fruit)
part of a plant that has seeds
Apples, oranges and grapes are all types of fruit.

fruit

fry (frying, fried)
to cook something using oil
Fry the fish until it is cooked.

fuzzy (fuzzier, fuzziest)
1 not clear
These pictures are fuzzy.
2 curly and soft
My hair is fuzzy.

How many things can you spot beginning with 'g'?

G g

game (games)
an activity with rules that you play for fun
What game shall we play?

garage (garages)
1 a building to keep a car
The garage is next to the house.
2 a place where cars are repaired
The car is at the garage.

gallop (galloping, galloped)
to run very fast, like a horse does
The horse galloped across the field.

garden (gardens)
land where flowers and plants can be grown
The garden is full of flowers.

galloping

abcdefghijklmnopqrstuvwxyz

gate (gates)
a door in a fence or wall
There is a gate between our garden and our neighbour's garden.

gentle
1 kind and careful not to hurt or disturb people or things
She is gentle with the animals.
2 not loud or strong
There is a gentle breeze blowing.

geography
the study of the Earth, countries and people
I like geography because we read about different people and places.

ghost (ghosts)
a dead person's spirit
Do you believe in ghosts?

giant (giants)
an imaginary person who is very big
The story is about a giant.

gift (gifts)
something given to someone, a present
That's a lovely gift, thank you.

giraffe (giraffes)
a very tall wild animal with a long neck
Giraffes live in Africa.

girl (girls)
a female child
There are 15 girls in our class.

girls

give (giving, gave, given)
to let someone have something
We gave our teacher a present.

glad (gladder, gladdest)
happy about something
He was glad to see us.

gift

glass (glasses)
1 hard, clear material that is used to make windows, bottles and mirrors
The bowl is made out of glass.
2 a container that you drink from
Can I please have a glass of water?

glasses
two pieces of glass or plastic that you wear to protect your eyes or to see better
I wear glasses for reading.

glitter
tiny pieces of sparkly material
We could make a birthday card and put glitter on it.

glitter (glittering, glittered)
to sparkle and shine brightly
Her necklace glittered in the sunlight.

globe

Puzzle time
Which of these objects is the odd one out?
glass
jar
bottle
plate
Answer: plate

globe (globes)
1 the world
He sailed around the globe.
2 a map of the world in the shape of a round ball
Turn the globe round to find Australia.

gloomy (gloomier, gloomiest)
1 dark
It's a gloomy day.
2 sad
Don't look so gloomy. Smile!

glove (gloves)
a piece of clothing to wear on your hands
You need your gloves today; it's cold.

glue
a thick liquid that sticks things together
Put a dot of glue in each corner of the picture.

glue (gluing, glued)
to stick things together
I'm going to glue these pictures in my scrapbook.

a b c d e f **g** h i j k l m n o p q r s t u v w x y z

a b c d e f **g** h i j k l m n o p q r s t u v w x y z

goal (goals)
1 the net and posts in a game such as football or hockey, where the player tries to place the ball
The goalkeeper stands in front of the goal.
2 the point given to a team when it puts the ball inside the goal
The striker scored another goal.
3 something you hope to do
My goal in life is to be a teacher.

goal

goat (goats)
a farm animal that usually has horns
Goats will eat almost anything.

gold
a valuable, yellow metal
The ring is made of gold.

goldfish (goldfish or goldfishes)
a small orange fish that people like to keep as a pet
I feed my goldfish once a day.

good (better, best)
1 of high quality
It's a very good school.
2 pleasant
I'm having a good time.
3 well-behaved
They have been really good children.

goodbye (bye)
something you say when you are leaving someone
Goodbye and good luck!

goose (geese)
a bird that looks like a big duck
There are geese on the farm.

goose pimples (goosebumps)
little bumps on your skin that appear when you are cold or frightened
I've got goose pimples on my arms.

gorilla (gorillas)
the biggest type of ape
We saw a huge gorilla at the zoo.

gorilla

GP (general practitioner; GPs)
a doctor who looks after the health of people in a local area
Mum took me to see the GP when I had earache.

grandfather

grandchild (grandson, granddaughter)
the child of your children
Grandparents love seeing their grandchildren.

grandchildren

grandparent (grandfather, grandmother)
the parent of your mother or father
Our grandparents live with us.

grape (grapes)
a small, round, juicy fruit that grows in bunches
Grapes can be green or purple.

grass
a green plant with thin leaves that grows over the ground
My brother is cutting the grass.

gravity
the force that pulls things towards the earth
Gravity is what makes things fall to the ground.

gravy
a brown, meaty sauce
I like gravy poured over mashed potato.

great
 1 very good
 This is a great song.
 2 very big
 There was a great storm.

greedy (greedier, greediest)
wanting or taking more food or money than is necessary
He was a greedy king.

grapes

ground
 1 the earth that is under your feet
 Lie on the ground and look up at the stars.
 2 a piece of land used for a purpose
 The football ground is on the edge of town.

a b c d e f **g** h i j k l m n o p q r s t u v w x y z

group (groups)
people or things
that are together
or connected
*The children are sitting
in groups of four.*

group

**guess (guessing,
guessed)**
to try to give the right
answer when you are
not sure if it is correct
Guess which hand it is in.

grow (growing, grew, grown)
to become bigger or longer
The flowers are growing very well.

guest (guests)
a person you invite to your house
*We've got some guests coming this
weekend.*

grown-up (grown-ups)
a child's word for a man or a
woman who is no longer a child
*Some grown-ups aren't very good
at using computers.*

guinea pig (guinea pigs)
a furry animal with no tail that
people keep as a pet
*We have a guinea pig in our
classroom.*

grumpy (grumpier, grumpiest)
in a bad mood
He's always grumpy in the morning.

guitar (guitars)
a stringed musical
instrument with a long neck
He plays the guitar in a band.

guard (guards)
a person who protects something
or someone
*Four guards stood outside
the palace.*

gun (guns)
a weapon that fires bullets
In the film the cowboy had a gun.

**guard (guarding,
guarded)**
to protect something
or someone
Soldiers guard the palace.

gym (gyms)
a place where people go to
exercise
*There are lots of different
machines at the gym.*

guitar

a b c d e f **g** h i j k l m n o p q r s t u v w x y z

How many things can you spot beginning with 'h'?

Hh

habit (habits)
something that you do often and do without thinking about it
Biting your nails is a bad habit.

habitat (habitats)
the place where an animal or plant lives in the wild
A frog's natural habitat is in or near a pond.

hailstones
little balls of ice that fall like rain from the sky
Hailstones the size of tennis balls sometimes fall in India.

hair

hair (hairs)
thin threads that grow on your skin and head
She has long, curly hair.

half

half (halves)
one of two equal parts
Would you like half an orange?

a b c d e f g **h** i j k l m n o p q r s t u v w x y z

hall (halls)
1 the room next to the main door of a house
I always take my shoes off in the hall.
2 a big room used for meetings or parties
We do PE in the hall.

hamster

ham
meat from a pig's leg
Would you prefer ham or cheese in your sandwich?

hamburger (hamburgers)
minced beef cooked and served in a round bun
We cooked hamburgers when we were at camp.

hammer (hammers)
a tool used for hitting nails into wood
Don't drop the hammer on your toe. It's heavy!

hammock

hammock (hammocks)
a piece of material that hangs between two poles or trees which is used as a bed
It's fun to swing in a hammock.

hamster (hamsters)
a small, furry animal like a mouse
Hamsters keep food in their cheeks.

hand (hands)
the part of your body at the end of your arm
Your fingers and thumb are attached to your hand.

handbag (handbags)
a bag used for keeping things in
Mum keeps a hairbrush and keys in her handbag.

handle (handles)
the part of a bag, door or jug that you hold on to
Hold the kettle by its handle.

handsome
nice-looking
He's a very handsome man.

hang (hanging, hung)
to attach the top part of something, leaving the lower part free or loose
The teacher hung my picture on the wall.

hangar (hangars)
a big building where aeroplanes are kept
There are lots of hangars at the airport.

hanger (hangers)
a curved piece of wood or plastic to hang clothes on
Pick your shirt up and put it on a hanger.

happen (happening, happened)
to be, to take place
What a lot of noise. What's happening?

hat

happy (happier, happiest)
feeling pleased
I'm happy because we're going on holiday tomorrow.

harbour (harbours)
a safe place for ships and boats near land
The fishing boats leave the harbour early in the morning.

hard
1 not soft
This bed is very hard.

2 difficult, not easy
The questions are very hard.

harvest (harvests)
the time of the year when farmers cut and collect crops that have been growing, or the crops themselves
The farmer had a good harvest of potatoes last year.

hat (hats)
a piece of clothing that you wear on your head
You must wear a hat in the sun.

hate (hating, hated)
to strongly dislike something or someone
Our cat hates going to the vet for her injections.

haunted
if a building is haunted people think ghosts live in it
Some people say that the house on the corner is haunted.

hay
dry grass which is cut and used to feed animals
Horses and cows eat hay.

a b c d e f g **h** i j k l m n o p q r s t u v w x y z

abcdefg**h**ijklmnopqrstuvwxyz

head (heads)
1 the part of your body above your neck
Put your hands on your head.
2 a person who is the leader
The head of the school has her own office.

headphones
things that cover or go into the ears and through which you can listen to music without other people hearing it too
I can never hear people talking to me when I'm wearing my headphones.

healthy (healthier, healthiest)
1 well and strong
My grandad walks 3 miles every day to keep healthy.
2 good for you
Fruit and vegetables are very healthy foods.

hear (hearing, heard)
to be aware of sounds by using your ears
Can you hear a noise?

heart (hearts)
1 the part of your body that pumps your blood
Your heart beats faster when you run.
2 the main part of something
The theatre is in the heart of the city.
3 a shape that means love
Valentine's cards often have hearts on them.

heart

heat (heating, heated)
to make something warm
Heat the soup but don't boil it.

heavy (heavier, heaviest)
weighing a lot
These books are heavy.

heavy

hedge (hedges)
a line of bushes along the side of a field or garden
The ball went over the hedge.

hedgehog (hedgehogs)
a small, wild animal with sharp hairs on its back
Hedgehogs curl up in a ball.

heel (heels)
1 the back part of your foot
Your heel is under your ankle.
2 the part of a shoe that is under your heel
Mum's shoes have high heels.

height
how tall something is
What is your height in centimetres?

height

helicopter (helicopters)
an aircraft with blades on top that spin and make it fly
The helicopter landed in the field.

hello
what you say when you see or meet someone, or when you answer the telephone
Hello! How are you?

helmet (helmets)
a hat that protects your head
Always wear a helmet when you ride your bike.

helmet

help (helping, helped)
to make it easier for someone to do something
Let me help you carry those books.

hen (hens)
a female chicken
Hens lay eggs.

hen

here
in this place
I like it here.

hibernate (hibernating, hibernated)
to sleep during cold weather
Some animals hibernate in winter.

hide (hiding, hid, hidden)
to put yourself or something out of sight
Hide the presents, she's coming.

high
1 how long something is from the bottom to the top
How high is the mountain?
2 a long way above
The plane is high above us.

a b c d e f g **h** i j k l m n o p q r s t u v w x y z

a b c d e f g **h** i j k l m n o p q r s t u v w x y z

hill (hills)
a high piece of ground
Run down the hill.

hippopotamus (hippo; hippopotamuses or hippopotami)
a large animal that lives near rivers and lakes in Africa
Hippos like to splash in mud.

hippo

history
things that have happened in the past
The history of our town is very interesting.

hit (hitting, hit)
to swing your hand or something you are holding against something else
Hit the ball as hard as you can.

hive

hive (hives)
a box where bees live and where they keep their honey
Thousands of bees live in each hive.

hobby (hobbies)
something that you enjoy doing in your spare time
My hobbies are skateboarding and listening to music.

hockey
a game played on a field by two teams that hit a ball using curved wooden sticks
We play hockey in winter and cricket in summer.

hold (holding, held)
to have something in your hands or arms
Hold my coat, please.

hole (holes)
an opening or an empty space
There's a hole in the bag.

holiday (holidays)
1 a special day
Easter is a religious holiday.
2 a time when you do not have to work or go to school
We're going on holiday next week.

hollow
empty inside
The log is hollow.

holly

a plant with shiny, prickly leaves and red berries
People use holly to make Christmas decorations.

holly

hologram (holograms)

a picture made with a laser
There is a hologram on the sticker.

home

the place where you live
What time will you get home?

homework

school work you do at home
I do my homework when I get home from school.

honey

honey

a sweet, sticky food made by bees
I like honey on my porridge.

hood (hoods)

a piece of clothing that covers your head, usually part of a coat or jacket
Put your hood up, it's raining.

hoof (hooves)

the foot of an animal, such as a deer, horse or goat
Horses have very thick hooves.

hook (hooks)

a piece of metal or plastic for hanging up or catching things
Hang your jacket on the hook.

hoof

hoop (hoops)

a large ring of metal, wood or plastic
It's fun to play with hoops.

hop (hopping, hopped)

to jump on one foot
I can hop across the room.

hope (hoping, hoped)

to wish for something
I hope you have a good time.

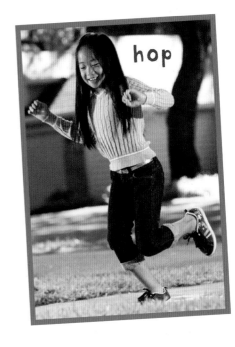
hop

a b c d e f g **h** i j k l m n o p q r s t u v w x y z

horizon
a line in the distance where the sky appears to touch the sea
You can see a boat on the horizon.

horn (horns)
1 one of the hard, pointed things on an animal's head
Bulls have horns.
2 part of a car that makes a loud noise
The driver beeped his horn.

horrible
bad or unpleasant
What a horrible colour.

horse (horses)
a large animal with four legs, a mane and a tail
My brother can ride a horse.

hospital (hospitals)
a place where sick or injured people go to get better
Have you ever stayed in hospital?

hot (hotter, hottest)
at a very high temperature
Egypt is a hot country.

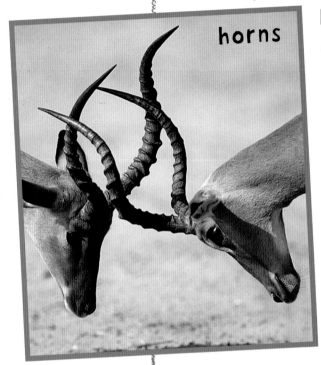
horns

hot dog (hot dogs)
a sausage in a long bun
Would you like a hot dog?

hotel (hotels)
a place people pay to stay in
We stayed in a hotel near the beach.

hour (hours)
sixty minutes
The television programme lasts an hour.

house (houses)
a building that people live in
My house is at the top of the hill.

house

housework
cleaning and other
jobs that need to be
done every day in
the house
*Most people hate
housework.*

hurricane

huge
very big
*There is a huge crowd waiting
outside.*

human (human being)
a person, not an animal
*My cat is cleverer than some
humans.*

hump (humps)
a large bump
*Some camels have two humps and
others have just one.*

hungry (hungrier, hungriest)
feeling that you need food
I'm hungry. What's for dinner?

hunt (hunting, hunted)
1 to look for something
or someone
*We hunted everywhere
for the other shoe.*

2 to try to catch
wild animals
*Owls hunt mice
at night.*

**hurricane
(hurricanes)**
a very strong
wind storm
*Hurricanes can cause lots of
damage.*

hurry (hurrying, hurried)
to do something quickly
*Hurry and get your coat, it's time to
go home.*

hurt (hurting, hurt)
1 to cause pain to someone
The injection won't hurt you.
2 to feel pain
My knee hurts.

husband (husbands)
A man who is married
Dad is Mum's husband.

hutch

hutch (hutches)
a box where pet
rabbits live
*I clean my rabbit's
hutch once a day.*

a b c d e f g h i j k l m n o p q r s t u v w x y z

a b c d e f g h i j k l m n o p q r s t u v w x y z

How many things can you spot beginning with 'i'?

Ii

ice
water that is so cold that
it has frozen and
become hard
*Let's go skating
on the ice.*

iceberg (icebergs)
a huge piece of ice
that floats in the sea
*We saw the tip of an
iceberg.*

iceberg

ice cream
a sweet, frozen food
that is usually made
from milk or cream
*Ice cream tastes
good on hot days.*

ice
cream

ice hockey
a game that two
teams play on ice.
Players use sticks to try to hit a
disc into the goal
*The rubber disc used in ice
hockey is called a puck.*

ice skate (ice skates)
a boot with a metal blade
on the bottom for moving
across ice
You can hire ice skates at the rink.

ice-skate (ice-skating, ice-skated)
to move across ice wearing ice skates
We're learning how to ice-skate.

icicle (icicles)
a thin, pointed stick of ice
There were icicles hanging from the roof.

icing
a sweet covering for cakes
Mum put chocolate icing on the cake.

icicles

idea (ideas)
a plan or a thought about how to do something
Have you any ideas about how we can raise money for the school outing?

identical
exactly the same
Tommy and Charlie are identical twins.

identical

igloo (igloos)
a house made of blocks of snow and ice
The Inuit people live in igloos in winter.

ill
not well, sick
He's feeling ill so is going to see the doctor.

imaginary
not real
The story is about an imaginary cat with magical powers.

imagine (imagining, imagined)
to make a picture of something in your mind
Try to imagine what life was like a hundred years ago.

imitate (imitating, imitated)
to copy
The children imitated the monkeys' behaviour.

immediately
now, at once, right away
Please put your clothes away immediately.

a b c d e f g h i j k l m n o p q r s t u v w x y z

important

1 serious, useful or valuable
It is a very important discovery.

2 powerful
The mayor is an important person in our town.

impossible

not able to be or to happen
That's impossible – you can't be in two places at once!

improve (improving, improved)

to get better
Your spelling is improving.

increase (increasing, increased)

to get bigger
The population of our town has increased a lot in the last ten years.

increase

infectious

if an illness is infectious other people can catch it easily
Measles is an infectious illness caused by a virus.

information

facts or knowledge about someone or something
There is a lot of information on our website.

impossible

initial (initials)

the first letter of a person's name
My initials are J M.

injection (injections)

a way of putting medicine into your body using a special needle
My baby sister had an injection yesterday.

injure (injuring, injured)

to hurt yourself or someone else
The footballer fell and injured his leg.

ink

coloured liquid that is used for writing or printing
Sign your name in ink.

innocent

an innocent person hasn't done anything wrong
He's not guilty; he's innocent.

insect (insects)
a small creature with six legs
Beetles, butterflies and bees are all types of insects.

insects

inside
in or into a place or container
Come inside the house; it's very cold out there.

instrument (instruments)
1 something people use to do a job
A stethoscope is an instrument that a doctor uses to listen to sounds in your body.
2 something that makes music
Guitars and violins are instruments.

instruments

Puzzle time
Can you find three insects hidden in this wordsearch?

t	r	b	e	e	o
s	d	l	e	f	w
e	u	a	y	a	a
c	a	n	d	d	s
a	e	t	r	o	p
z	x	c	t	n	o

Answers: ant bee wasp

interactive
an interactive computer program allows users to change things
In this interactive game you click on the ball to try to score a goal.

interested
wanting to pay attention to something or someone so that you can learn more
Sam is interested in sport.

interesting
exciting in a way that keeps your attention
This book is really interesting.

Internet
a huge system of linked computers all over the world that lets people communicate with each other
We use the Internet at home and at school.

a b c d e f g h **i** j k l m n o p q r s t u v w x y z

a b c d e f g h **i** j k l m n o p q r s t u v w x y z

interrupt (interrupting, interrupted)
to stop someone who is speaking
The phone call interrupted our conversation.

invade (invading, invaded)
to attack or go into a place in large numbers
The Vikings invaded Britain in the 8th century.

invent (inventing, invented)
to make something that has not been made before
The Chinese invented paper nearly 2000 years ago.

invention (inventions)
something new that someone makes, or produces, for the first time
The scientist is working on her new invention.

investigate (investigating, investigated)
to examine something carefully to find out the truth about it
The police are still investigating the burglary.

iron

invisible
not possible to see
You can't read it, it is written in invisible ink!

invitation (invitations)
a note or a card that asks you to go to a party
Have you replied to the party invitation?

invite (inviting, invited)
to ask someone to come somewhere with you
Ellie always invites lots of people to her parties.

iron
1 a strong, hard metal
The spade is made of iron.
2 (irons) a machine for making clothes smooth
Be careful! The iron gets very hot.

island (islands)
a piece of land that has water all around it
There's a small island in the middle of the lake.

island

How many things can you spot beginning with 'j'?

J j

a b c d e f g h i **j** k l m n o p q r s t u v w x y z

jail (jails)
a prison, a place where people
are kept by the police
*The thief was put in jail for seven
months.*

jam
a sweet food made from fruit
We have toast and jam for breakfast.

jacket (jackets)
a short coat
*Take a jacket with you;
it might be cold.*

jar (jars)
a glass container for storing
food
Jam and honey are sold in jars.

jars

jackpot (jackpots)
the biggest prize
in a lottery or
competition
*If I win the jackpot
I'll buy you a
present.*

jealous
feeling angry or bad because you want something that someone else has
He is jealous because I got a prize.

jeans
trousers made of denim, a strong material
My favourite clothes are jeans and a T-shirt.

jeans

jeep (jeeps)
an open vehicle that is used for driving over rough ground
It was a bumpy ride in the jeep.

jelly (jellies)
a clear, sweet solid food made from fruit juice
We had jelly and ice cream at the party.

jellyfish (jellyfish or jellyfishes)
a sea creature with a soft, clear body that may sting
It's difficult to see jellyfish in the water.

jet (jets)
a fast aeroplane
The pop star flew to America in a private jet.

jewel (jewels)
a stone that is very valuable, such as a diamond or ruby
The crown was covered in beautiful jewels.

jewels

jewellery
necklaces, bracelets and earrings that you wear for decoration
My mum likes to wear jewellery.

jigsaw (jigsaws)
a puzzle made from pieces that fit together to make a picture
The jigsaw has 100 pieces.

jellyfish

job (jobs)
1 work that you get paid for doing
She has a new job at the hospital.
2 something that you have to do
It's my job to take out the rubbish.

jockey (jockeys)
someone who rides a horse in a race
The winning jockey collected her prize.

jog (jogging, jogged)
to run slowly for exercise
My dad jogs three miles every morning.

jockey

join (joining, joined)
1 to become a member of a club or other group
I've joined the chess club.
2 to stick or fasten together
Join the two pieces of card with sticky tape.

joke (jokes)
a funny story that makes people laugh
Do you know any good jokes?

jolly (jollier, jolliest)
happy, always smiling
He's a jolly person.

journey (journeys)
a trip from one place to another
We were very tired after the long journey.

judge (judges)
1 the person in a court who says how to punish a guilty person
Judges often wear wigs in court.
2 a person who chooses the winner in a competition
The judges gave him nine points.

judge (judging, judged)
to say how good something is
The headmistress is going to judge the art competition.

Puzzle time

Look at this joke. Use the code to find out what the answer is.

A	B	C	D	E	F	G	H	I	J
1	2	3	4	5	6	7	8	9	10

K	L	M	N	O	P	Q	R
11	12	13	14	15	16	17	18

S	T	U	V	W	X	Y	Z
19	20	21	22	23	24	25	26

What did one road say to the other?
13/5/5/20 25/15/21 1/20 20/8/5
3/15/18/14/5/18!

Answer: Meet you at the corner!

a b c d e f g h i **j** k l m n o p q r s t u v w x y z

a b c d e f g h i **j** k l m n o p q r s t u v w x y z

judo
a Japanese fighting sport
In judo people try to throw each other to the floor.

jug (jugs)
a container with a handle for liquids
Fill the jug with water.

juice   jug

juggle (juggling, juggled)
to throw several things up in the air and catch each one quickly without dropping them
The acrobat juggled with four balls.

juice
liquid from fruit or vegetables
You can have orange juice or apple juice.

jump

jump (jumping, jumped)
to push yourself off the ground with both feet
Jump as high as you can.

jumper (jumpers)
a piece of warm clothing that covers your upper body that you pull over your head
My granny knitted me a jumper.

jungle (jungles)
a thick forest in a hot country
The trees and plants in a jungle grow very close together.

junior
for younger people
I play in the junior orchestra.

junk
things you don't want any more because they are old or no good
The garage is full of junk.

just
1 happened a very short time ago
I've only just arrived.
2 exactly the right amount or thing
There was just enough flour to make a cake.
3 only
No, it's not a fly. It's just a bit of fluff.

How many things can you spot beginning with 'k'?

K k

kaleidoscope (kaleidoscopes)
a tube with pictures or pieces of
coloured glass or plastic at one
end that you look through and
turn to see changing patterns
*The kaleidoscope was
invented in 1816.*

kaleidoscope

**kangaroo
(kangaroos)**
an Australian
animal that keeps
its young in a
pouch on the front
of its body
*Kangaroos have big,
strong back legs.*

kangaroo

karaoke
the playing of the music of songs
without the words, so people can
sing the words into a microphone
Karaoke started off in Japan.

karate
a Japanese fighting sport
*In karate you fight using your
hands and feet.*

a b c d e f g h i j **k** l m n o p q r s t u v w x y z

a b c d e f g h i j **k** l m n o p q r s t u v w x y z

kebab (kebabs)
pieces of meat or vegetables on
a stick
Let's have a takeaway kebab.

keep (keeping, kept)
1 to continue to have something
*You can keep the books for two
weeks.*
2 to continue to do something
Don't keep staring at that man.
3 to store something in a certain
place
We keep the paints in the cupboard.

kennel (kennels)
a small structure, usually made
out of wood, for a dog to sleep in
*The man next door is making a
kennel for his dog.*

kick

ketchup
a thick, cold, sauce
made out of tomatoes
*I'd like some ketchup on my
burger, please.*

kettle (kettles)
a container with a lid for boiling
water
*Come in. I'll put the kettle on and
make some tea.*

key

key (keys)
1 a piece of
metal used to
open a lock
Have you seen my door key?
2 one of the parts of a computer
or piano that you press with your
fingers
*Type the file name and then press
the 'enter' key.*
3 a set of answers or an
explanation of symbols
There is a key at the back of the book.

keyboard (keyboards)
the set of keys on a computer or
a piano that you press to type or
make a sound
*This is a special keyboard with
letters and pictures.*

**kick (kicking,
kicked)**
to swing your foot
at something
*Kick the ball into
the goal!*

kill (killing, killed)
to cause someone or
something to die
Some weeds kill other plants.

kind
helpful, pleasant and
thoughtful
*It's very kind of you
to think of me.*

king (kings)
a royal man who
rules a country
*Do you think the prince
will become king?*

king

kiss (kissing, kissed)
to touch someone with your lips
Mum kissed us all goodnight.

**kitchen
(kitchens)**
the room in
a house for
preparing food
*There are nice
smells coming from
the kitchen.*

kite (kites)
a toy for flying in the air, made
of light wood and cloth, paper or
plastic and that has a long string
Shall we fly the kite today?

kite

kitten (kittens)
a baby cat
*Our cat has just
had a litter of
kittens.*

**kiwi fruit
(kiwi fruits)**
a green fruit
with a brown,
hairy skin
*Mum sliced a kiwi fruit to
put in the fruit salad.*

kitten

knee (knees)
the part of your leg that bends
*When you walk, you
bend your knees.*

Puzzle time
How many kitchen things can
you find in this word puzzle?

sinkbathovencupboardtable
chairsofashelfcupbedsaucer

Answer: 8

**kneel (kneeling,
knelt)**
to get down on
your knees
*Dad knelt down to
stroke the cat.*

knife (knives)
a tool with a blade
for cutting
things into pieces
*Use a knife to cut
the meat.*

a b c d e f g h i j **k** l m n o p q r s t u v w x y z

knight (knights)
a type of soldier who lived hundreds of years ago
Knights wore armour when they rode into battle.

knight

knit (knitting, knitted)
to make clothes or other things using wool and two long needles
Jodie knitted a scarf.

knob (knobs)
1 a round handle on a door, cupboard or drawer
I opened the drawer and the knob came off in my hand.
2 a round switch on a radio or on a machine
Turn the knob to make it louder.

knock (knocking, knocked)
to hit something to make a noise
Someone is knocking on the door.

knot (knots)
the place where two pieces of string or rope are tied together
There's a knot in my shoelaces.

know (knowing, knew, known)
1 to have information and facts in your mind
I know that Rome is the capital of Italy.
2 to have met someone before or be familiar with them
Do you know our neighbour Mrs Smith?

knuckle (knuckles)
one of the bony places in your hand where the fingers bend
When you make a fist you can see your knuckles.

koala (koalas)
an Australian animal that looks like a small grey bear
Koalas live in trees.

koala

a b c d e f g h i j k **l** m n o p q r s t u v w x y z

How many things can you spot beginning with 'l'?

L l

label (labels)
a piece of paper or cloth that gives information about the thing it is attached to
Always put a label on your folders.

lace
fine cloth made with patterns of tiny holes
The doll's dress is made of lace.

ladder (ladders)
a piece of equipment made from two long bars joined together by short bars, which you climb to reach high places
Dad uses a ladder when he paints the house.

ladybird (ladybirds)
an insect that is red with black spots
Ladybirds are good for the garden.

ladybird

lake

lake (lakes)
a big area of water that has land all around it
There are lots of rowing boats on the lake.

lamb

1 (lambs) a young sheep
Lambs are born in the spring.
2 meat from lambs
We had roast lamb for dinner.

lamb

lamp (lamps)

a light that you can carry around
I have a lamp on my desk.

land

1 ground
They built a house on a plot of land.
2 the dry part of the Earth
The sailors were happy to see land.
3 (lands) a place or a country
The castle is in a magical land.

land (landing, landed)

to reach the ground after being
in the air
The plane lands at 2:45 p.m.

language (languages)

words people use when they
speak and write
French and English are languages.

lap (laps)

1 the top of your legs when you
are sitting down
My cat sits on my lap.

2 once around a track
They ran 12 laps of the track.

laptop (laptops)

a small computer that you can
carry around with you
*Some people use
laptops on trains.*

laptop

large

big
*We ate a
large piece of cake.*

larva (larvae)

a very young form of an insect
*The larva of a butterfly is called a
caterpillar.*

laser (lasers)

a powerful light or the machine
that makes it
*Doctors
sometimes
use lasers in
operations.*

lasso

lasso (lassos)

a long rope with a
loop at one end
*The cowboy used a lasso
to round up all the cattle.*

a b c d e f g h i j k **l** m n o p q r s t u v w x y z

last

1 after the others

We came last in the egg and spoon race.

2 the most recent, the one that happened the shortest time ago

We went to Italy for our last holiday.

last (lasting, lasted)

to continue to work or to happen

How long do you think this good weather will last?

late

1 after the normal or correct time

Sorry I'm late!

2 towards the end of a period of time

It was late on Sunday afternoon when we left for town.

laugh (laughing, laughed)

to make a sound that shows you are happy, or when you think something is funny

We laughed at Dad's silly joke.

law (laws)

a rule made by the government

There are laws about children working before the age of 14.

lawn (lawns)

an area of grass that is kept short in a garden or a park

We play football on the lawn.

lay (laying, laid)

1 to put in a place

Lay out your pencils in a row.

2 to make an egg

The hens lay eggs most days.

lazy (lazier, laziest)

1 not wanting to work

Don't be lazy. Get up out of the armchair.

2 not busy, relaxed

We had a nice, lazy weekend.

lead (leads)

a strap that you put on a dog when taking it for a walk

Please keep your dog on a lead!

lead (leading, led)

1 to show someone the way

The guide led us through the cave's passageways.

2 to be in the front

The black horse is leading the race.

a b c d e f g h i j k **l** m n o p q r s t u v w x y z

leaf

leaf (leaves)
one of the many flat, green
things on a plant or tree
Dad swept up all the leaves.

lean (leaning, leant, leaned)
1 to bend your body
Lean over to reach the ball.
2 to rest against something
Chris was leaning against the wall.

leap (leaping, leapt)
to jump into the air
or over something
*The fish leapt out
of the water.*

leap

**learn (learning,
learnt, learned)**
to get knowledge or information
about a subject
We are learning French at school.

leather
the skin of an animal that is used
to make bags, shoes and other
things
My belt is made of leather.

leave (leaving, left)
1 to go away from a place
What time are you leaving?

2 to put a thing in a place or
to let a thing stay in a place
You can leave your bike here.

leg (legs)
1 the part of your body between
your hip and your foot that you
stand on
You've got longer legs than me.
2 the part of a table or chair that
holds it up
One of the chair legs is broken.

legend (legends)
a very old story about things that
happened a long time ago
*There are many legends about
Robin Hood.*

lemon (lemons)
a yellow fruit with a sour taste
I put a slice of lemon in my drink.

lemonade
a cold, sweet, fizzy drink
We drank lemonade at the party.

lend (lending, lent)
to let someone have or use
something that they will return
after using
Could you lend me a pen, please?

length
how long something is
This table is one metre in length.

leopard (leopards)
a wild cat with yellow
fur and black spots
*Leopards are fast runners
and can climb trees.*

leopard

leotard (leotards)
a stretchy piece of clothing like a
swimming costume with sleeves
We wear leotards to do ballet.

lesson (lessons)
a time when you are learning
something from a teacher
We had two lessons in the morning.

let (letting, let)
1 to allow someone to do
something
Will your mum let you come over?
2 to allow something to happen
Just let the ball drop.

letter (letters)
1 one of the signs of the alphabet
used in writing
*There are five letters in the word
'catch'.*

2 a written message that you put
in an envelope and send or give
someone
*You can either send a
letter or an email.*

lettuce (lettuces)
a green, leafy vegetable
eaten in salads
We're growing lettuce this year.

library (libraries)
a place where you can borrow
books
*A mobile library comes to our
village twice a week.*

lick (licking, licked)
to put your tongue
on something
lick
Lick your ice cream, it's going to drip.

lie (lies)
something you say that you know
is not true
I told a lie and said I liked her dress.

lie (lying, lay, lain)
to have your body flat on the
floor, ground or bed
*We put our towels on the sand and
lay down.*

a b c d e f g h i j k l m n o p q r s t u v w x y z

a b c d e f g h i j k **l** m n o p q r s t u v w x y z

lie (lying, lied)
to say something that you know is not true
They lied about their age.

life
1 (lives) the time between when you are born and when you die
He had a long and happy life.
2 the state of being alive
Is there is life on other planets?

lifeboat (lifeboats)
a boat that helps people who are in danger at sea
The lifeboat rescued the fishermen just in time.

lifeboat

lift (lifts)
1 a machine that takes you up and down in a building
Take the lift to the fourth floor.
2 a ride in a car
Do you need a lift?

lift (lifting, lifted)
to move something to a higher place
It took four people to lift our piano.

lift

light
1 energy or brightness from the Sun or a lamp that lets you see things
Is it light enough to take a photo?
2 (lights) a device with a bulb that gives out light
Turn off the light, it's time for bed.

light (lighter, lightest)
not heavy
My bag is light because there's nothing in it.

lighthouse (lighthouses)
a tower on the coast that has a bright light that flashes to warn ships
There's a lighthouse at the end of the beach.

lightning
electrical light in the sky during a storm
We could see lightning in the distance.

like (liking, liked)
1 to enjoy something or be fond of someone or something
I really like skateboarding.

2 to want
What would you like for your birthday?

limb (limbs)
an arm or a leg
I felt dizzy and all my limbs were shaking.

line (lines)
1 a long, thin mark
Draw a line through the mistakes.
2 a piece of string, rope or wire
Hang the clothes on the line.
3 a row
There is a line of trees by the park.

lion (lions)
a large wild cat that lives in Africa
Male lions have long hair on their head called a mane.

lion

lip (lips)
one of the two edges of your mouth
The cat came in, licking his lips.

liquid (liquids)
something, such as water that and can be poured
Milk, juice and water are liquids.

listen (listening, listened)
to pay attention to sound
Are you listening to me?

litter

litter
1 rubbish lying on the ground
We picked up all the litter.
2 (litters) the group of babies that an animal has at one time
Our dog had a litter of puppies.

little
1 small, not large
My little brother is so funny.
2 not much
We gave the cat a little milk.

live (living, lived)
1 to be alive
My uncle lived to be 90 years old.
2 to have your home in a certain place
They live in France now.

living room (living rooms)
a room in a house for sitting and relaxing in
The TV is in the living room.

a b c d e f g h i j k **l** m n o p q r s t u v w x y z

a b c d e f g h i j k **l** m n o p q r s t u v w x y z

lizard (lizards)
a small reptile with a long tail
Lizards have dry, scaly skin.

lizard

llama (llamas)
an animal from
South America
that has a soft, woolly coat
Llamas can carry heavy loads.

loaf (loaves)
bread that is baked in one piece
*Get a loaf of bread from
the shop.*

loaf

lobster (lobsters)
a sea creature with
eight legs and two claws
*We saw a lobster through
the glass-bottomed boat.*

lock (locks)
an object that closes something
that you can only open with a key
There's a lock on the diary.

lock (locking, locked)
to close or fasten
something with a key
*Have you locked the
door?*

lock

locker (lockers)
a narrow metal cupboard
We left our suitcase in a locker.

loft (lofts)
the inside of the roof of a house
There's some old books in the loft.

log (logs)
a thick piece of a tree
It's cold. Put another log on the fire.

lollipop (lollipops)
a hard, round sweet on a stick
I bought an orange lollipop.

lonely (lonelier, loneliest)
feeling sad that you are alone
Old people sometimes get lonely.

long
1 measuring a big distance from
one end to the other
We sit at a long table for lunch.
2 continuing for a large amount
of time
It's a very long film.

look (looking, looked)
to pay attention to
something that you see
Look at that hot-air balloon.

loose
1 not tight
These trousers are loose.
2 escaped, free
loose
The bull is loose in the field.

lorry (lorries)
a large vehicle for carrying things
My uncle drives a big lorry.

lose (losing, lost)
1 not to be able to find something
I've lost my key.
2 not to win a competition or a game
Our team lost the match.

lottery (lotteries)
a game where you can win a big prize if the numbers on your card match the winning numbers
If I win the lottery I'll buy a car.

loud
not quiet, making a lot of noise
There was loud music coming from upstairs.

loud

love (loving, loved)
to like someone or something very much
We love our new baby.

lovely (lovelier, loveliest)
beautiful or pleasant
It's a lovely day.

low
close to the ground, not high
The Sun was low in the sky.

lucky (luckier, luckiest)
1 fortunate, having good things happen to you
They're lucky they won the lottery.
2 giving good luck
These are my lucky football boots.

luggage
the bags and suitcases you take with you when you are travelling
I can't carry all this luggage.

lunch (lunches)
a meal that you eat in the middle of the day
What's for lunch today?

lung (lungs)
one of two parts of your body inside your chest that help you to breathe
Your two lungs are protected by bones called ribs.

a
b
c
d
e
f
g
h
i
j
k
l
m
n
o
p
q
r
s
t
u
v
w
x
y
z

a b c d e f g h i j k l **m** n o p q r s t u v w x y z

How many things can you spot beginning with 'm'?

Mm

macaroni
pasta shaped like small tubes
I like macaroni with cheese sauce.

machine (machines)
a piece of equipment
that is used to
do a job
*Washing
machines
wash, rinse and
spin your clothes.*

magazine (magazines)
a thin book with a paper cover
containing pictures and stories
*My mum buys her favourite
magazine every week.*

magic
a power to make strange things
happen
The coin disappeared by magic.

magician (magicians)
a person who does magic tricks
We had a magician at my party.

magnet (magnets)
a piece of metal that makes
some other metal objects
move towards it
A magnet will pick up all these pins.

magnet

magpie (magpies)
a big, black-and-white bird with a long tail
Magpies sometimes steal shiny objects.

magpie

mail
all the letters, cards and parcels you send or receive in the post
He sat at his desk reading his mail.

main
the most important or the biggest
We'll meet you in front of the main entrance.

make (making, made)
1 to create or build something
I made a model of an aeroplane.
2 to cause something to happen or be a certain way
That joke always makes me laugh.

male (males)
a man, boy or an animal that cannot produce eggs or have babies
The male peacock is the one with the big, colourful tail.

mammal (mammals)
a type of animal that gives birth to live babies and makes milk for them to drink
The elephant is the largest land mammal.

mammal

man (men)
an adult male
A man knocked at the door.

many (more, most)
large in number
I've been to France many times.

map (maps)
a drawing that shows where things and places are in a building, town, country or other place
We studied a map of the world.

marble
1 a type of hard stone
The statue is made of marble.
2 (marbles) a small glass or metal ball used to play a game
I won two marbles in that last game.

marbles

march

march (marching, marched)
to walk with regular steps
The soldiers marched in the parade.

mark (marks)
1 a sign or shape
Put a mark to show where your house is.
2 a letter or number that a teacher puts on a piece of work to show how good it is
She's getting good marks this term.
3 a spot or a dark patch on something that makes it look bad
There is a mark on the carpet where we spilled the juice.

market (markets)
a place where you can buy food, clothes, plants and other things
Most markets are outdoors.

marmalade
jam that is made from oranges
My mum likes toast and marmalade.

marry (marrying, married)
to become husband and wife
They married three years ago.

mask (masks)
something that you put over your face to hide or protect it
She wore a mask to go to the fancy-dress party.

mast (masts)
a tall pole on a boat that holds up the sail
The pirate climbed up the mast.

mat (mats)
a piece of material, like a small carpet, that you put on the floor
Wipe your feet on the mat.

match (matches)
1 a small stick that makes a flame when you rub it against something rough
We have special long matches for lighting the fire.
2 a contest or game
That's the best tennis match I've ever seen.

match

match (matching, matched)
to go well together or be the same
Does my shirt match my trousers?

mathematics (maths)
the study of numbers or shapes
Mathematics is my favourite subject at school.

mattress (mattresses)
the soft, thick part of a bed that you sleep on
My mattress is too hard and I can't get to sleep.

mayonnaise
a cold, thick, creamy sauce that you put on salads
Could I have mayonnaise in my sandwich, please?

mayor (mayors)
the leader of the town or city council
The mayor came to our autumn fair.

maze (mazes)
a lot of confusing paths that it is difficult to find your way through
We couldn't find our way out of the maze, but it was fun.

meadow

meadow (meadows)
a field with grass and flowers
There are lots of pretty flowers growing in the meadow.

meal (meals)
the food you eat at certain times of the day
Our main meal was roast chicken.

meal

mean
1 cruel or unkind
Don't be mean to each other.
2 not wanting to spend money
The king is very mean and counts his money every day.

mean (meaning, meant)
1 to explain something or say what something is
What does this word mean?
2 to want or plan to do something
I didn't mean to hurt him.

a b c d e f g h i j k l **m** n o p q r s t u v w x y z

a b c d e f g h i j k l **m** n o p q r s t u v w x y z

meaning (meanings)
the information that you get
from words and signs
*Can you explain the meaning
of this sentence?*

measles

measles
a serious illness
that that can give
you a high temperature and lots
of red spots
*When we had measles, we had to
stay in bed.*

measure

**measure
(measuring,
measured)**
to find out the
size or amount of something
We measured the line with a ruler.

meat
food that comes from the bodies
of animals
*Chicken, beef and pork are all types
of meat.*

mechanic (mechanics)
a person who fixes cars and
machines
*My dad works as a mechanic at the
garage.*

medal (medals)
a piece of metal that is given as
a prize for winning a competition
or for doing something special
He won a medal for bravery.

medicine
1 something that you take
when you are not well so that
you will get better
*You have to take this medicine
three times a day.*
2 the study of illness and injury
*She is studying
medicine because
she wants to be a
doctor.*

medium
middle sized, between large and
small
I'd like a medium popcorn, please.

meet (meeting, met)
1 to get to know someone for the
first time
*I met my best friend Theo on the
first day of school.*
2 to go to the same place as
another person
*Let's meet at 10 o'clock in front of
the swimming pool.*

melody (melodies)
a song or the tune of a song
The song has a strange but beautiful melody.

melon (melons)
a large fruit with a hard skin and flat seeds
Melons can be green, yellow or orange.

melt

melt (melting, melted)
to change from a solid to a liquid when the temperature rises
The ice in my drink has melted.

memory (memories)
1 something that you remember from the past
Photographs bring back memories.
2 the ability to remember things
Do you have a good memory?
3 the part of a computer where information is stored
This computer has more memory than our old one.

mend (mending, mended)
to repair
Could you help me mend the tyre?

menu (menus)
1 the list of food in a café or restaurant
The waiter brought us each a menu.
2 a list of things seen on a computer screen
Click here to go back to the main menu.

menu

mermaid (mermaids)
in stories, a sea creature with a woman's body but a fish's tail instead of legs
The mermaid was sitting on a rock combing her hair.

message (messages)
information for a person from someone else
I sent you a message by email.

messy (messier, messiest)
untidy
This room is very messy.

metal
hard material such as gold, silver, copper or iron
Coins are made out of metal.

metal

microphone (microphones)
something that is used for recording sounds or making them louder
Sing into the microphone.

microphone

microscope (microscopes)
something that makes small things look much bigger
We looked at a hair under the microscope.

microwave (microwaves)
an oven that cooks food very quickly
Heat the soup in the microwave.

midday
12:00 in the middle of the day
We'll have our lunch early – at about midday.

middle (middles)
the centre or the part of something that is halfway between the beginning and the end
We sat down in the middle of the row.

midnight
12:00 in the middle of the night
We stay up until midnight on New Year's Eve.

mild
1 not too strong or serious
She had a mild case of flu.
2 not tasting too strong or too spicy
It's a mild curry.
3 not too cold, quite warm
The weather is mild today.

milk
white liquid that female mammals produce to feed their babies
The milkman leaves two pints of milk on the doorstep every day.

milk

mime (miming, mimed)
to act or tell a story without using any words
The children mimed scenes from the story.

mind (minds)
the part of you that helps you think and remember
I said the first thing that came into my mind.

mind (minding, minded)
1 not to like something, or to be worried by it
I don't mind what we play.
2 to be careful
Mind your head when you go through the door.
3 to look after something or someone
I'll mind your cat while you're on holiday.

mind

minus
1 the sign used in maths when taking one number away from another
Twenty-five minus five equals twenty.
2 in temperature, below zero
It's cold today, it's minus one outside!

minute (minutes)
sixty seconds
We waited for twenty minutes but they didn't come.

miracle (miracles)
a wonderful thing that happens that you can't explain
It's a miracle that no one was killed in the plane crash.

mirror

mirror (mirrors)
special glass in which you can see your reflection
Go and look in the mirror; you look really pretty.

miserable
very unhappy
Don't look so miserable.

miss (missing, missed)
1 not to hit a target
He threw the ball but missed the basket.
2 to feel sad because you are not with someone
My dad is away in the army and I miss him.

mist
light fog caused by tiny drops of water forming a cloud near the ground
The mist soon cleared and the sun came out.

a b c d e f g h i j k l **m** n o p q r s t u v w x y z

mistake (mistakes)
something that is wrong
If you make a mistake, cross it out.

mitten (mittens)
a glove that does not have separate places for each finger
Wrap up well and wear your mittens.

mix (mixing, mixed)
to put different things together and stir them
Mix the eggs and sugar together.

moat (moats)
a ditch or deep hole around a castle
The people in the castle built the moat to keep out their enemies.

moat

mobile phone (mobile phones)
a small telephone that people carry around
Call me on my mobile phone.

model (models)
1 a small copy of something such as a plane or a building
We made a model of a jet plane at the weekend.

2 a person whose job is to show clothes
She wants to be a model.
3 one type of something
This computer is the most up-to-date model.

money
coins and paper that you use to buy things
Have you spent all your money already?

monitor (monitors)
1 the part of a computer that shows the screen
It's easier to see on a big monitor.
2 a pupil who has a special job to do
I'm the book monitor this term.

monkey (monkeys)
an animal with a long tail that is good at climbing trees
We watched the monkeys at the zoo.

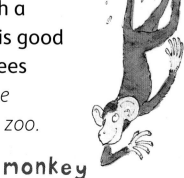

monkey

monster (monsters)
a frightening creature
in stories and films
*The monster chased
them into the forest.*

monster

month (months)
one of the twelve parts of the
year
*June and July are
summer months.*

Moon

moon (Moon; moons)
the round shining
object that you see in
the sky at night
*The Moon goes round the Earth and
takes four weeks to go round once.*

mop (mops)
a sponge or lots of strips of cloth
on the end of a handle that you
use for cleaning floors
*Put the mop back in the bucket
when you've finished.*

more (most)
1 stronger or greater than
*This book is more interesting than
the one I was reading last week.*

2 a bigger amount or number
Is there any more cake?

morning (mornings)
the part of the day between the
time the sun comes up and noon
*We get up at the same time every
morning.*

mosque (mosques)
a building where Muslims pray
*Ali goes to the mosque every
Friday.*

moth (moths)
an insect that looks like a
butterfly
Moths fly around at night.

mother

mother (mothers)
a woman who has
a child or a female
animal that has
young
*My mother
looks after me.*

motor (motors)
the part of a machine that uses
power to make it work
*The washing-machine motor is
broken.*

a b c d e f g h i j k l **m** n o p q r s t u v w x y z

a b c d e f g h i j k l **m** n o p q r s t u v w x y z

**motorbike
(motorcycle;
motorbikes,
motorcycles)**
a vehicle with two
wheels and an
engine
*Dad has a new
motorbike.*

**motorway
(motorways)**
a road where cars
can drive fast and
travel a long way
*There aren't any traffic lights or
roundabouts on a motorway.*

mountain (mountains)
a very high piece of land, bigger
than a hill
*Some mountains have snow on top
all year round.*

mouse

mouse (mice)
1 a small animal with
a long tail and a pointed nose
There are mice in the field.
2 part of a computer that you
click on to move things around
on the screen
You need a mouse to play this game.

Puzzle time
Spot five differences
between these two pictures

**moustache
(moustaches)**
the hair that grows
above a man's lip
*My dad has a little
moustache.*

mouth (mouths)
the part of your
face with lips, teeth
and your tongue
*You talk and eat
using your mouth.*

move (moving, moved)
to change your position or the
position of something else
*Can you move your head, please?
I can't see.*

movie (movies)
a film, a story that is told using
pictures that move
Let's watch a movie tonight.

much (more, most)
a lot
Thank you so much for coming.

mud
wet soil or earth
I'm covered in mud!

mug (mugs)
a big cup with tall sides
Do you want a mug of hot chocolate?

mugs

multiply (multiplies, multiplying, multiplied)
to add a number to itself, often more than once
What number do you get if you multiply two by four?

music

munch (munches, munching, munched)
to eat something noisily
The rabbit munched on carrots.

muscle (muscles)
one of the parts of the body that tightens and relaxes to cause movement
My brother has got big muscles because he goes to the gym.

museum (museums)
a place where old, important, valuable or interesting things are kept so that people can go and look at them
There is a toy museum in our town.

mushroom (mushrooms)
a small fungus with a stem with a round top that you can eat
Do you want mushrooms on your pizza?

music
a pattern of sounds that is sung or played on special instruments
The orchestra played such beautiful music.

must
to have to do something
You must put your books away.

mustard
a yellow or yellowish-brown sauce that tastes hot and spicy
I'd like mustard on my hot dog.

mysterious
strange, secret or difficult to understand
He is a mysterious person; we don't know much about him.

myth (myths)
a very old story about gods, goddesses and heroes
The story Pandora's Box is an ancient Greek myth.

a b c d e f g h i j k l **m** n o p q r s t u v w x y z

a b c d e f g h i j k l m **n** o p q r s t u v w x y z

How many things can you spot beginning with 'n'?

Nn

nail (nails)
1 a thin, sharp piece of metal with one flat end that you hit with a hammer
Hammer a nail into the wall so we can hang up the picture.
2 the hard covering on the ends of your fingers and toes
He bites his nails.

nail

name (names)
what a person or object is called
What's your name?

name

narrow
having only a short distance from one side to the other
The road is very narrow.

nasty (nastier, nastiest)
very unpleasant or bad
That's a very nasty cut.

nation (nations)
a country and the people who live there
Teams from all nations take part in the Olympic Games.

national
to do with a country
or the whole country
We waved the national
flag of our country.

national

nature
all the animals, plants, rivers,
mountains and other things in
the world that are not made by
people
I like reading books about nature.

naughty (naughtier,
naughtiest)
badly behaved
Don't be naughty.

near
close by, not far
There's a bus stop near the zoo.

neat
clean or organized
His room is always neat and tidy.

necessary
if something is necessary you
really need it or it must be done
It's useful to have your own
computer, but it isn't necessary.

Puzzle time
Someone has been very
naughty and written this
message backwards. Can
you work out what it says?

uoy dluohs od ruoy
krowemoh yreve yad

Answer: you should do your
homework every day

neck (necks)
the part of your
body that attaches
your head to your
shoulders
Put a scarf around
your neck.

necklace
(necklaces)
a piece of jewellery
that you wear
around
your
neck
That's a
beautiful
necklace.

naughty

navy (navies)
the ships and people that fight
for a country at sea during a war
My cousin is in the navy.

necklace

a b c d e f g h i j k l m **n** o p q r s t u v w x y z

nectarine (nectarines)
a fruit like a peach but with a smooth skin
This nectarine is lovely and juicy.

need (needing, needed)
if you need something, you must have it
I need another exercise book; this one is full.

needle

needle (needles)
1 a thin, sharp piece of metal with a hole through it used for sewing
Could you thread this needle for me, please?
2 a thin, sharp piece of metal through which injections are given
The needle will not hurt you.

neighbour (neighbours)
a person who lives near you
We invited all our friends and neighbours to the party.

nephew (nephews)
the son of your sister or brother
My nephew is staying with us for a few days.

nerve (nerves)
part of your body like a long string, which carries messages between the brain and other parts of the body
There are millions of nerves in the human body.

nervous
worried or frightened, not able to relax
She's a little nervous about being in the school play.

nest (nests)
a place birds make to lay their eggs
There's a robin's nest in that tree.

net (nets)
material that is made by joining pieces of string or thread together, leaving spaces between them
We use a small net when we go fishing.

nest

netball

a game played by two teams of seven players, usually women or girls. The aim is to throw a ball through a net hanging on a pole

My hobbies are netball and swimming.

nettle (nettles)

a wild plant whose leaves sting if you touch them

You can make tea and soup from nettles.

nettle

network (networks)

a system of things or people that are connected

This computer is part of a network.

never

not at any time, not ever

I've never been to China.

new

recently made or bought, not old

I love your jacket. Is it new?

new

news

information about something that is happening now or that happened a short time ago

Write soon and send us all your news.

newspaper (newspapers)

large sheets of paper which tell you what is happening in the world

newspapers

Have you read today's newspaper?

next

1 the one that is nearest to you

There's an empty seat next to Susie.

2 the one that is immediately after someone or something else

Who's next on the list?

nice

enjoyable, good, pleasant

Did you have a nice time?

nickname (nicknames)

a name which your friends and family call you

My brother Rory's nickname is Rozza.

a
b
c
d
e
f
g
h
i
j
k
l
m
n
o
p
q
r
s
t
u
v
w
x
y
z

a b c d e f g h i j k l m **n** o p q r s t u v w x y z

niece (nieces)
the daughter of your sister or brother
Her niece works in a bank.

night (nights)
the time between sunset and sunrise, when it is dark
You can see the stars on a clear night.

nightdress (nightie; nightdresses, nighties)
a dress to sleep in
Put your nightdress on and get into bed.

nightdress

nightmare (nightmares)
a bad dream
Nightmares can be very scary.

nil
a score of nothing in sport
Our team won four-nil.

nobody
no one, no person
There's nobody home.

nod (nodding, nodded)
to move your head up and down
You can nod your head instead of saying 'yes'.

noise (noises)
a loud sound
Did you hear that noise?

noisy

noisy (noisier, noisiest)
very loud or making a lot of noise
There were lots of noisy people on the beach.

none
not any, not one
I wanted some bread but there was none left.

nonsense

nonsense
something that does not make any sense, or mean anything
The idea that animals can drive is complete nonsense.

no one
nobody, not one person
I have no one to talk to.

noodles
long, thin strips of pasta
Do you want rice or noodles with your beef?

noodles

noon
midday, 12:00
The bell goes at noon.

normal
something that is ordinary or usual
It's normal to feel tired first thing in the morning.

nose (noses)
the part of your face that you use for breathing and smelling things
Breathe in deeply through your nose.

nose

nostril (nostrils)
one of the two openings at the bottom of your nose
The horse wrinkled its nostrils and tossed its head back.

note (notes)
1 a short written message
Mum wrote a note to the school.
2 a piece of paper money
This machine doesn't take notes.
3 a musical sound or the mark to show a musical sound
She played three notes on the piano.

nothing
not anything, zero
There's nothing in the box; it's empty.

notice (notices)
a sign that tells people something
The notice says that the play starts tomorrow.

notice (noticing, noticed)
to see something, or be aware that it is there
Did you notice if anyone was in the shop?

novel (novels)
a book that tells a long story
Her latest novel is about a family in India.

a b c d e f g h i j k l m **n** o p q r s t u v w x y z

a b c d e f g h i j k l m **n** o p q r s t u v w x y z

now
this time, the present
My dad used to work in a factory, but he works at home now.

nowhere
not anywhere
There's nowhere else to go.

number (numbers)
1 a word or symbol that you use when you count things
Some people think seven is a lucky number.
2 the group of numbers you press when you phone someone
What's your mobile number?

nurse (nurses)
a person whose job is to look after people who are sick or hurt
The nurse put a bandage on my finger.

Puzzle time

What are the missing words in these nursery rhymes?

1. Jack and Jill went up the – – – –
2. Humpty – – – – – – sat on a wall
3. Mary, Mary, quite – – – – – – – –

Answers: 1. hill 2. Dumpty 3. contrary

numbers

nursery (nurseries)
1 a place where small children are looked after while their parents are at work
My little brother goes to nursery.
2 a place where people grow and sell plants
My dad bought some strawberry plants at the nursery.

nursery rhyme (nursery rhymes)
a poem or song for young children
My favourite nursery rhyme is Humpty Dumpty.

nut (nuts)
a seed that you can eat
Peanuts, cashews and almonds are all different types of nuts.

nuts

How many things can you spot beginning with 'o'?

oasis (oases)
an area in the desert where there is water and where trees and plants grow
There are lots of oases in the Sahara desert, but you might travel for days without seeing one.

oak (oaks)
a big tree with seeds called acorns
That oak is over two hundred years old.

oar (oars)
a pole which is wide and flat at one end that you use when you row a boat
I let go of the oar and it fell into the water.

oak

ocean
1 the salt water that covers most of the Earth
Strange fish live at the bottom of the ocean.
2 (oceans) a large sea
The Pacific is the largest ocean in the world.

a b c d e f g h i j k l m n **o** p q r s t u v w x y z

a
b
c
d
e
f
g
h
i
j
k
l
m
n
o
p
q
r
s
t
u
v
w
x
y
z

octopus (octopuses)
a sea creature that has eight legs
The legs of an octopus are called tentacles.

octopus

off
1 away from somewhere
Take the glass off the table.
2 not in use, not switched on
Switch the computer off if you're finished with it.

office (offices)
a place where people work at desks
There are four people in my mum's office.

ogre

ogre (ogres)
a frightening giant in stories
The ogre roared until the mountains shook.

oil
1 a thick liquid made from plants or animals and used for cooking
Pour a little oil into the pan.
2 a thick liquid that comes out of the ground and is used to make petrol
They discovered oil there last year.

3 a thick liquid that is used on metal or wood so that parts move better or more easily
This door is squeaking. Can you put some oil on it, please?

okay (OK)
1 fine, healthy, well
Are you okay?
2 all right
Is it okay if I copy my work to your computer?

old
not young, not new
We live in an old house.

once
1 one time
We've met only once before.
2 one time in a fixed period
We go swimming once a week.

onion (onions)
a vegetable that has a strong smell and taste
Peeling onions makes you cry.

online
using the Internet
I bought these trainers online.

open
not closed or covered over
They must be at home; all the windows are open.

open (opening, opened)
1 to move a door or window so it is no longer closed
We opened the window because it was too hot.
2 to let customers in to buy things
What time does the shop open?

open

operation (operations)
when a doctor cuts open a person's body to mend or remove something
I've got to have an operation on my eye.

opponent (opponents)
the person you are playing against in sport
In judo you try and throw your opponent to the ground.

opposite
1 completely different
The opposite of near is far.

2 across from, facing
They live in the house opposite the garage.

orange
1 (oranges) a round, juicy fruit with a thick skin
Oranges are much sweeter than lemons.
2 the colour between red and yellow
She's wearing an orange jacket.

orbit (orbiting, orbited)
to travel round and round something, like a planet in space
The Earth orbits the Sun.

orchestra (orchestras)
a group of people playing musical instruments together
He plays the violin in the school orchestra.

order (ordering, ordered)
1 to ask for something in a restaurant or shop
Can I order a coffee, please?
2 to tell someone what to do
The captain ordered the men to attack the ship.

a b c d e f g h i j k l m n o p q r s t u v w x y z

a b c d e f g h i j k l m n **o** p q r s t u v w x y z

ordinary
nothing special, normal
It's just an ordinary house.

ostrich (ostriches)
a large, African bird with a
long neck
Ostriches cannot fly.

ostrich

otter (otters)
a brown,
furry wild
animal that swims and eats fish
Otters feed mainly at night.

out
1 away from
The mouse got out of his cage.
2 not at home
She's out at the moment.

outdoors
not inside a building, in the open
air
It's much cooler outdoors.

oven (ovens)
something that you use to bake
or roast food
*Bake the cake in the oven for
45 minutes.*

over
1 above, on top of
We live over a cake shop.
2 finished, ended
Is the film over yet?
3 from one side to another
She crossed over the road.

**overtake (overtaking,
overtook, overtaken)**
to go past someone or something
It's dangerous to overtake on a bend.

owl (owls)
a bird that hunts at night
*Sometimes you can
hear an owl hooting.*

**own
(owning, owned)**
to have something
that you bought or
were given
We own our house.

owl

oxygen
a gas that animals and plants
need to live
Fire needs oxygen in order to burn.

How many things can you spot beginning with 'p'?

P p

a b c d e f g h i j k l m n o **p** q r s t u v w x y z

paddle (paddling, paddled)
1 to move a boat through water using oars or your hands
I paddled the dinghy across the lake.
2 to walk in shallow water
My little brother can't swim yet, but he likes to paddle.

paddling

padlock (padlocks)
a type of lock with a metal loop that fastens things together
I chained my bike to the railings with a padlock.

pack (packing, packed)
to put things into boxes, bags or suitcases
Don't forget to pack your suitcases.

package (packages)
a small parcel
This package has your name on it.

page (pages)
one side of a sheet of paper in a
book, magazine or newspaper
This book has 192 pages.

pain (pains)
the feeling you have when you
are hurt or ill
I have a bad pain in my side.

paint (paints)
a sticky liquid that
you brush onto things
to colour them
Don't spill paint on the carpet.

paint

pair (pairs)
1 two things that go together
I need a new pair of trainers.
2 something that is made of two
similar things joined together
*I've bought a new pair of sunglasses
for my holiday.*

palace (palaces)
a big house where a king, queen
or other important person lives
The princess lived in an old palace.

palm (palms)
1 the inside part of your hand
Fortune tellers read palms.

2 a kind of tree with leaves only
at the top
*Our tent was under a row of palms
on the beach.*

pan (pans)
a round cooking pot
Fry an egg in the pan.

pan

**pancake
(pancakes)**
a thin, flat cake
that is cooked in
a frying pan
I like pancakes with sugar.

panda (pandas)
a large, black-and-white animal
that is part of the bear family
Pandas come from China.

pantomime (pantomimes)
a funny musical show that is
performed around Christmas
The pantomime this year is 'Aladdin'.

paper
1 thin sheets of material for
writing or printing on
There is no paper in the printer.
2 (papers) a newspaper
My dad buys a paper every day.

parachute (parachutes)
a piece of equipment made of cloth that people wear to let them fall slowly through the air
The parachute opens automatically.

parade (parade)
a lot of people walking or marching in a long line to celebrate a special occasion
There is a parade every year.

parade

parcel (parcels)
something which is wrapped up in paper and often sent in the post
My parcel arrived today.

parent (parents)
a mother or father
My parents are both dentists.

park (parks)
a piece of ground with trees and grass
Let's go to the park to play.

park (parking, parked)
to put a car or bike in a place for a time
You can park in front of the library.

parrot (parrots)
a bird with coloured feathers that usually lives in hot countries
My parrot can say my name.

parrot

part (parts)
1 one of the pieces or sections that something is divided into
Would you like part of my newspaper?
2 the role of an actor in a film or a play
Who is playing the part of the princess?

partner (partners)
a person you work or do something with
Will you be my partner for this dance?

party (parties)
a group of people who meet to enjoy themselves
I'm having a party on Saturday.

a b c d e f g h i j k l m n o **p** q r s t u v w x y z

abcdefghijklmnopqrstuvwxyz

pass (passing, passed)
1 to go beyond or past a person, place or thing
You'll pass the bakery on your way.
2 to succeed in doing something such as a test or an examination
I hope you pass your driving test.
3 to give someone something
Could you please pass the salt?

passengers

passenger (passengers)
someone who travels in a vehicle that is driven by someone else
This coach has seats for 48 passengers.

Passover
a Jewish holiday held in the spring
The family get together for Passover.

passport (passports)
a little book that shows who you are, that you need when you travel to another country
You have to show your passport at the airport.

past
1 after a certain hour
Let's meet at half past six.
2 on the far side of something
The bank is on this street, just past the supermarket.
3 the time before the present
In the past, email didn't exist.

pasta
food made from flour, eggs and water, cut into shapes
We had pasta with tomato-and-mushroom sauce for lunch.

pasta

paste
1 a type of glue
I made a paste of flour and water.
2 a soft, spreadable mixture
He likes fish paste on his sandwiches.

patch (patches)
1 a small piece of material to cover a hole in something
I put a patch on my jeans.

2 a small area which is different from the area around it
There are damp patches on the wall.

patient (patients)
a person who is in hospital or visiting a doctor
This car park is for patients only.

patient
able to wait without complaining or getting bored
Please be patient! Dinner will be ready soon.

patio (patios)
an area outside a house with paving stones instead of grass
We sometimes have our meals on the patio.

pattern (patterns)
1 lines, shapes or colours arranged in a certain way
The dinner plate has a pattern painted on it.
2 a shape that you copy or use as a guide to make something
Mum used a pattern to make this jacket for me.

pattern

pavement (pavements)
the path you walk on next to a road
Be sure to walk on the pavement.

paw (paws)
the foot of an animal
Our dog has a sore paw.

paw

pay (paying, paid)
to give someone money for something that you are buying, or because someone has done work for you
I'll pay for the theatre tickets now.

peas

pea (peas)
a small, round green seed that is eaten as a vegetable
I had fish, chips and peas for dinner.

peace
1 no war or fighting
There has been peace between them for many years.
2 quiet, calmness
She needed a little peace and quiet.

a b c d e f g h i j k l m n o **p** q r s t u v w x y z

peach (peaches)
a soft fruit with a large seed inside it
This is a sweet, juicy peach.

peacock

peacock (peacocks)
a male bird with long, brightly coloured tail feathers that spread out like a fan
Peacocks usually have green and blue feathers.

peanut (peanuts)
a small nut with a soft, bumpy shell
You can buy salted peanuts in small packs.

pear (pears)
a fruit with green skin that grows on a tree and that is narrow at the top and wide at the bottom
We had pears with chocolate sauce for dessert.

pebble (pebbles)
a small, smooth, round stone
We threw pebbles into the sea.

pedal (pedals)
1 part of a bicycle that you push with your feet to make the wheels go round
Can you reach the pedals?
2 part of a car that you push with your feet to make it stop and go
The middle pedal stops the car.

peel
the skin on fruit and vegetables
You can eat the peel of an apple.

peel (peeling, peeled)
to take the skin off a fruit or a vegetable
I peeled the potatoes for lunch.

peel

peg (pegs)
1 a clip for fastening clothes to a washing line
Clothes pegs are made of wood or plastic.
2 a small hook where you can hang things
I hung my coat up on a peg.

pen (pens)
an object for drawing and writing with ink
Sign this with a black pen.

pencil (pencils)
an object with a sharp point used for drawing and writing
I drew the outline using a pencil.

pen

pencil

penguin (penguins)
a black-and-white sea bird that cannot fly
Penguins are brilliant at swimming.

people
human beings; men, women and children
There were a lot of people in town today.

pepper
1 a hot powder used to flavour food
Please pass the salt and pepper.
2 (peppers) a sweet or hot-tasting vegetable
Peppers can be green, red, yellow or orange.

peppers

perfume (perfumes)
a liquid with a pleasant smell that you put on your skin
What perfume are you wearing?

person (people, persons)
a human being; a man, woman or child
Our geography teacher is a very interesting person.

pet (pets)
an animal that is kept at someone's home
Do you have any pets?

pets

petal (petals)
one of the coloured parts of a flower
Daffodils have yellow petals.

petrol
liquid fuel that makes a car engine run
We need to stop for petrol.

phone (phones)
a telephone
Be quiet! I'm on the phone.

a b c d e f g h i j k l m n o **p** q r s t u v w x y z

a b c d e f g h i j k l m n o **p** q r s t u v w x y z

phone (phoning, phoned)
to call someone
on the telephone
*Joe phoned while
you were out.*

pickle

**photo
(photograph;
photos, photographs)**
a picture made with a camera
*We had our photos taken for our
passports.*

phrase (phrases)
a group of words coming
together
*The phrase 'a piece of cake' means
easy.*

piano

piano (pianos)
a large musical
instrument with
black and white keys
I play the piano.

pick (picking, picked)
1 to choose
The teacher picked me for the team.
2 to break off a flower or a piece
of fruit from a plant
We picked blackberries in the woods.

pickle (pickles)
vegetables in vinegar which keep
fresh for a long time
I like cheese and pickle at lunchtime.

picnic (picnics)
food that you take outdoors to
eat
We had a picnic in the park.

picture (pictures)
a drawing, painting or
photograph
The best picture will be in the paper.

pie (pies)
food made with fruit, vegetables,
fish or meat that is baked inside
pastry
Would you like another piece of pie?

piece (pieces)
a part of something that
has been separated or
broken
*Careful! There are some
pieces of glass on the floor.*

pig (pigs)
a farm animal with
pink skin and a curly tail
A baby pig is called a piglet.

pig

pigeon (pigeons)
a grey bird that lives in towns
Please don't feed the pigeons!

pile

pile (piles)
a lot of things put on
top of each other
*There's a pile of
washing on the floor.*

pillow (pillows)
a cushion to put your
head on in bed
I put my tooth underneath my pillow.

pilot (pilot)
the person who is in
control of a plane
*The pilot showed us the
plane's control panel.*

pilot

pin (pins)
a sharp, thin piece of metal that
is used to fasten things or hold
pieces of cloth together
*Take all the pins out before you try
the shirt on.*

pin

pinch (pinching, pinched)
to squeeze between your thumb
and fingers
Ow! He pinched my arm.

pineapple (pineapples)
a brown fruit that is yellow inside
and has pointed leaves that stick
out of the top
*This slice of pineapple is
very juicy.*

pirate (pirates)
a person who goes
onto boats and ships
to steal the things
they are carrying
*The ship was attacked by a group of
pirates.*

**pitch
(pitches)**
a piece of
ground painted
with lines where
you can play football,
hockey or another sport
Fans ran on to the pitch.

pizza (pizzas)
a thin, flat round bread that is
covered with tomatoes, cheese
and other toppings then baked in
an oven
*We're going to have pizza at the
party.*

a b c d e f g h i j k l m n o **p** q r s t u v w x y z

a b c d e f g h i j k l m n o **p** q r s t u v w x y z

place (places)
1 a town, area or building
What's the name of the place where we went on holiday last year?
2 a point or position
I broke my arm in two places.

plain
1 made of one colour, having no pattern or decoration
The curtains are plain green.
2 easy to understand
Can you tell me in plain English?
3 not fancy or complicated
It's a plain room, but very clean and neat.

plan (plans)
1 an idea about what will happen in the future
What are your plans for the weekend?
2 a drawing of a room, building or other space
We drew a plan of our playground.

plan (planning, planned)
to think about what you want to do and how to do it
Let's plan what we're going to do this weekend.

plane (planes)
an aeroplane
The plane took off from the airport on time.

plane

planet (planets)
one of the very large, round objects that moves around the Sun
Venus and Mars are planets.

plant

plant (plants)
a living thing that has roots, leaves and seeds and can make its own food
Water the plants every day.

plant (planting, planted)
to put seeds or plants into the ground or containers so they will grow
Plant the seeds in early summer.

plaster
1 a thick paste that hardens when it dries
The builder spread plaster on the walls.
2 (plasters) a thin piece of plastic or cloth that you put over a cut or sore
The nurse put a plaster on my knee.

plastic
a light material that is made from chemicals
The bucket is made of plastic.

plastic

plate (plates)
a flat dish to eat food from
Take the plates into the kitchen.

play (plays)
a story performed by actors in a theatre or on the radio
I hope I get a part in the school play.

play (playing, played)
to do things that you like such as games or sports
Let's play outdoors.

play

playground (playgrounds)
a place for children to play
There are swings and a slide at the playground.

please
a word to use when you are asking for something politely
Please wait here.

plenty
enough or more than enough
There are plenty of sandwiches, so take two.

plough (ploughs)
a piece of equipment that farmers use to turn the soil before they plant
Modern ploughs can cut through the earth very quickly.

plug (plugs)
1 a piece of plastic or rubber that stops water going out of a sink or bath
Put the plug in the bath, then turn on the water.
2 a piece of plastic connected to an electrical wire that you put into a wall
Which one is the plug for the computer?

plum (plums)
a small, red, green or purple fruit with a stone
We had plums and custard for dessert.

plums

a b c d e f g h i j k l m n o **p** q r s t u v w x y z

plumber (plumbers)
a person whose job it is to fix water taps and pipes
The plumber repaired the leak.

plus
and, added to, the symbol +
Eleven plus six equals seventeen;
11 + 6 = 17.

pocket (pockets)
a small, flat bag sewn into a piece of clothing or luggage
Put your key in your pocket.

poem (poems)
writing that uses words that sound good together. The words often rhyme
This poem is very funny.

point (points)
1 a sharp end on something
Use a pencil with a sharp point.
2 a certain place or time
There's a meeting point at the airport.

3 the reason for something
The whole point was to raise money for the school.
4 a mark for counting a score in a game
The answer is worth one point.

point (pointing, pointed)
to use your hand or finger to show where something is
Point to where the gate is.

poison (poisons)
something that will kill you or make you very ill if you swallow it
In the film the cook put poison in the soup.

Puzzle time
Can you unscramble the lines of this poem?

a. Roses red are
b. are blue Violets
c. sweet is Sugar
d. And are you so

Answer:
a. Roses are red
b. Violets are blue
c. Sugar is sweet
d. And so are you

poisonous

poisonous
harmful, containing poison
Some wild mushrooms are poisonous.

polar bear (polar bears)
a large, white bear that lives near the North Pole
Polar bears hunt fish and seals.

polar bear

pole (poles)
a long narrow piece of wood,
plastic or metal
We forgot to take the tent poles.

police
people whose job it is to make
sure everyone obeys the law
*Do you think we need to call the
police?*

polite
speaking or acting in a pleasant
and not rude way
*It is polite to say please, thank you
and excuse me.*

pollen
yellow or orange
powder found
inside flowers
*Bees carry pollen
from one flower to
another.*

pollen

pond (ponds)
a small area of water
There are fish in the pond.

pony (ponies)
a small horse
I had a ride on a pony.

pool (pools)
1 a place filled with water for
swimming
*I like playing in my pool when the
weather is warm.*
2 a puddle or another small area
of water
*We saw tiny fish in the pools on the
beach.*

poor
1 not having enough money
It's a very poor country.
2 not as good as it should be
The food was poor.

pop
1 (pops) a sudden noise
*There was a loud pop
when they opened the
bottle.*
2 a short form of
popular
*They are a famous pop
band.*
3 a fizzy drink
Do you want a bottle of pop?

poppy

poppy (poppies)
a wild, red flower with
black seeds
The field is full of poppies.

a
b
c
d
e
f
g
h
i
j
k
l
m
n
o
p
q
r
s
t
u
v
w
x
y
z

a b c d e f g h i j k l m n o **p** q r s t u v w x y z

popular
liked by a lot of people
Fishing is a popular hobby.

porcupine (porcupines)
a wild animal with long sharp
hairs like needles on its back
Some porcupines can climb trees.

pork
meat from a pig
*We had roast
pork and apple
sauce for dinner.*

potato

porridge
a warm breakfast
food that is made from oats
I like honey on porridge.

postcard (postcards)
a small piece of card with
a picture on one side.
You write on the other
side.
*I sent my grandparents
a postcard.*

poster (posters)
a large picture or notice that you
put up on the wall
I've posters on my bedroom wall.

post office (post offices)
a place where people buy stamps
and send letters and parcels
*Can you get me some stamps at the
post office?*

potato (potatoes)
a roundish white vegetable that
grows under the ground
Let's have baked potatoes for lunch.

pour (pouring, poured)
to make a liquid move out of or
into something
Pour the milk into the jug.

powerful
1 very strong
*A powerful tornado swept through
town.*
2 able to control other people
and things that
happen
*It is one of the most
powerful countries in
the world.*

powerful

practice
something that you do again and
again to get better at something
What time is swimming practice?

practise (practising, practised)
doing something regularly to improve a skill
Keep practising your serve.

pram (prams)
a little bed on wheels for moving a baby around
I'm taking the baby out in the pram.

prefer (preferring, preferred)
to like something better than another thing
I prefer apple juice to lemonade.

prepare (preparing, prepared)
to get ready or to make something ready
I'm preparing for the test.

presents

present
1 (presents) a gift, a thing that you are given without asking for it
Thank you for all the presents.
2 now
The story is set in the present.

president (presidents)
the leader of an organization or a country
She is president of the club.

press (pressing, pressed)
to push something
Press the button on the machine.

pretend (pretending, pretended)
to act like something is true when it is not
She pretended to be asleep.

pretty (prettier, prettiest)
nice to look at
What pretty flowers!

price (prices)
the amount of money that something costs
The prices are high.

prince (princes)
the son or grandson of a king or queen
The prince rode through the forest.

princess (princesses)
the daughter or granddaughter of a king or queen
The princess dreamt of a faraway place.

princess

print (printing, printed)
1 to put letters, numbers or pictures on paper with a machine
Print five copies of the story.
2 to write words without joining the letters
Print your name in full.

printer (printers)
1 a machine connected to a computer that makes copies on paper
The printer is out of paper.
2 a person who prints books, newspapers, leaflets and other things
Take the poster to the printer.

prison (prisons)
a place where people are kept under guard as punishment
The thief was sent to prison.

prison

private
only for some people, not for everyone
The beach is private; it belongs to the hotel.

prize (prizes)
something that you win in a game or competition
First prize is a gold trophy.

prize

problem (problems)
something that is wrong and needs to be corrected
We have a problem.

programme (programmes)
1 a show on the radio or television
This is my favourite programme.
2 a thin book that tells you about a play or a show at the theatre
I'll look in the programme to see what the actor's name is.

promise (promises)
something you say you will definitely do
I always keep my promises.

promise (promising, promised)
to tell someone that you will definitely do something
Daniel promised his dad that he would behave at school.

a b c d e f g h i j k l m n o **p** q r s t u v w x y z

protect (protecting, protected)
to take care of someone or something and not let it be hurt or damaged
Penguins protect their chicks.

proud
feeling happy that you or someone else has done something
My parents are proud of me.

public
for everyone
The public transport in this town is very good.

puddle (puddles)
a little pool of water on the ground or floor
There are puddles after the rain.

puddle

pull (pulling, pulled)
to move something towards you or drag something behind you
The puppy pulled its blanket on the floor.

pull

pump (pumps)
a machine that pushes a liquid or gas from one place to another
Take your bicycle pump with you.

pumpkin (pumpkins)
a big, round, orange vegetable
The children made a lantern out of a pumpkin.

pumpkin

puncture (punctures)
a hole made by a sharp object, especially in a tyre
We had a puncture on the way home.

punish (punishing, punished)
to do something bad or unpleasant to someone because they have done something wrong
Don't punish him. It was an accident.

pupil (pupils)
1 a child that goes to school
The pupils wear a dark blue uniform.
2 the black circle in the middle of your eye
Your pupil gets smaller when you look at a bright light.

a b c d e f g h i j k l m n o **p** q r s t u v w x y z

puppet (puppets)
a toy that people move by putting their hand inside it or by pulling strings attached to it
Pinocchio is a puppet at the beginning of the story.

puppy (puppies)
a young dog
Puppies love to play.

puppets

pure
not mixed with anything else
This is pure apple juice.

purr (purring, purred)
to make a soft, low sound like a happy cat
Our cat purrs when you stroke her.

purse (purses)
a little bag to keep money in
I'll have to pay you later; I left my purse at home.

push (pushing, pushed)
1 to move something away from you or out of the way
He pushed past everyone.
2 to press down on something such as a key or a button
Push the restart button.

put (putting, put)
to move a thing to a place
Put the bags in the corner.

pyjamas
loose clothes that you wear to bed
Have a bath and put on your pyjamas.

pylon (pylons)
a tall, steel tower that holds up electricity wires
You see more pylons in the country than in towns.

pyramid (pyramids)
1 a very old stone building with triangular walls that form a point at the top
The Egyptian pyramids were built 4000 years ago.
2 something with this shape
The tent is shaped like a pyramid.

python (pythons)
a large snake that kills animals for food by squeezing them
Some pythons are eight metres long.

python

How many things can you spot beginning with 'q'?

Qq

quack (quacking, quacked)
to make the loud sound a duck makes
The ducks quacked when they saw me coming.

quarrel (quarrels)
an angry argument
The quarrel started over whose turn it was.

quarter (quarters)
one of four equal, or nearly equal, parts of something
Divide the apple into quarters.

queen (queens)
the royal female ruler of a country or the wife of a king
The queen lives in a palace.

queen

question (questions)
something that you ask someone
We'll try to answer all your questions.

a b c d e f g h i j k l m n o p q r s t u v w x y z

question mark (question marks)
a sign like this ? that you write at the end of a sentence
You need a question mark at the end of a sentence that begins with the word 'why'.

quilt

2 calm and still, not busy
The lake is quiet and peaceful at this time of day.

quilt (quilts)
a warm cover for a bed
Patchwork quilts are made by sewing lots of small pieces of cloth together.

queue (queues)
a line of people waiting
There was a long queue at the cinema.

quit (quitting, quit)
to stop doing something or to leave a computer program
To quit, press Ctrl + Q.

quiche (quiches)
a tart that is filled with eggs, cheese and vegetables, meat or fish
There's bacon in this quiche and salmon in that one.

Puzzle time
Can you answer all the questions in this quiz?
1. What is a baby pig called?
2. Can penguins fly?
3. Is a tomato a fruit or a vegetable?
4. What are the spines on a porcupine called?

Answers: 1. piglet 2. no 3. fruit 4. quills

quiz (quizzes)
a game or competition that tests your knowledge
Shall we see if we can answer the questions in the quiz?

quick
fast, taking a short time
Email is quick and easy.

quote (quoting, quoted)
to repeat the words that someone else has said or written
The English teacher quoted a line from one of Shakespeare's plays to the class.

quiet
1 not making a noise
Please be quiet.

a b c d e f g h i j k l m n o p q r s t u v w x y z

How many things can you spot beginning with 'r'?

a b c d e f g h i j k l m n o p q **r** s t u v w x y z

Rr

rabbit (rabbits)
a small furry animal with long ears
There are rabbits living in the wood.

rabbit

race (races)
1 a competition to see who can do something the fastest
The race starts in 15 minutes.

2 a group of people with similar physical features
People of all races and beliefs can live together happily.

race

race (racing, raced)
1 to take part in a race
There were ten drivers racing in the opening heats.
2 to do something very quickly
Jessica raced through the first part of the test.

racket

racket (rackets)

1 a flat, hard net on the end of a stick that you use to play some sports

Hit the ball hard with the racket.

2 a lot of loud noise

Who's making that racket?

radio (radios)

a piece of equipment that receives sounds

I listen to the radio in the car.

raft (rafts)

a simple flat boat made of pieces of wood tied together

They crossed the river on a raft.

rail (rails)

1 a metal or wooden bar that you can hang things on

I hang my clothes on the rail in my wardrobe.

2 one of two metal tracks that a train runs on

They put new rails along the track.

railway (railways)

1 a train track

The railway runs to the coast.

2 a system of trains

A railway is being built in the city.

rain

water that falls from clouds in the sky

Look at that heavy rain!

rain

rain (raining, rained)

when it rains, small drops of water fall from clouds in the sky

It's raining so we can't play outside.

rainbow (rainbows)

the curve of colours that you see in the sky after it rains and the sun comes out

The colours of the rainbow are red, orange, yellow, green, blue, indigo and violet.

raise (raising, raised)

to lift or put something in a higher place

Raise your hand if you know the answer.

Ramadan
the ninth month of the Muslim year
Muslims do not eat or drink during the day in the month of Ramadan.

raspberry (raspberries)
a small, soft, red fruit
I like raspberries with ice cream.

raspberries

rat (rats)
an animal that looks like a big mouse with a long tail
There are rats in the barn.

rattle (rattles)
a toy that makes a knocking noise when you shake it
Babies like playing with rattles.

raw
not cooked
Raw vegetables make a healthy snack.

rats

read (reading, read)
to understand words printed on a page
The teacher is reading to the class.

recipe (recipes)
a set of instructions telling you how to cook something, and what you need to make it
Can I have the recipe for this cake?

record (recording, recorded)
to write down or tape information
We recorded a song on the computer.

recorder (recorders)
a small musical instrument that you blow to make music
I play the recorder in the orchestra.

recycle (recycling, recycled)
to use something again
We're recycling newspapers and magazines at school.

referee (referees)
a person who makes sure that players in a game don't break the rules
The referee blew his whistle.

a b c d e f g h i j k l m n o p q **r** s t u v w x y z

reflection (reflections)
an image, like a copy of
something, that you
see in a mirror
or in water
*The dog
saw its reflection
in the pond.*

reflection

rehearsal (rehearsals)
a time when actors or singers
practise before appearing in
front of an audience
There's a rehearsal at lunchtime.

reindeer (reindeer)
a deer with big antlers that lives
in cold countries
Reindeer live in groups called herds.

relative (relatives)
a person in your family
We have relatives staying overnight.

**remember (remembering,
remembered)**
1 to keep information about the
past in your mind
I remember our holiday last year
2 to bring back information to
your mind
I've just remembered; my dad is out.

remind (reminding, reminded)
to cause someone to remember
something
Remind me to buy sugar.

repeat (repeating, repeated)
to say or do something again
Please repeat the question

reptile (reptiles)   reptile
a cold-blooded animal
with dry, scaly skin
Lizards are reptiles.

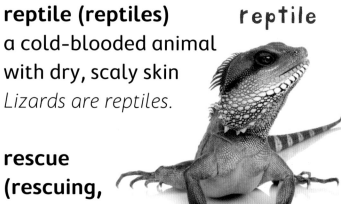

**rescue
(rescuing,
rescued)**
to save someone or something
from danger
The lifeguard rescued the children.

rest
1 a period of time when you relax
or do nothing
I'm tired. Let's have a rest.
2 the other things or people that
are left
You can have the rest of the sweets.

rest (resting, rested)
to relax, to sit or lie still
I wasn't asleep; I was just resting.

restaurant (restaurants)
a place where people eat and pay for meals
A new Thai restaurant has opened.

result (results)
1 something that happens because of something else
This beautiful garden is the result of a lot of hard work.
2 a final score
Have you heard the football results?

return (returning, returned)
1 to come back or go back to a place
He returned after the meeting.
2 to give or send something back
We returned the book to the library.

rhinoceros

rhinoceros (rhino; rhinoceroses)
a big, wild animal with thick skin and one or two horns on its nose
There are rhinos in Africa and Asia.

rhyme (rhyming, rhymed)
to end with the same sound as another word
Hat rhymes with cat.

ribbon (ribbons)
a narrow piece of material for tying up presents or decorating things
She's wearing ribbons in her hair.

rice
grains from a plant that are boiled and eaten as food
We had rice with our curry.

rice

rich
1 having a lot of money
Switzerland is a rich country.
2 food that has butter, cream and eggs is rich food
The cheese sauce is too rich for me!

riddle (riddles)
a difficult but funny question or puzzle
I know lots of jokes and riddles.

ride (riding, rode, ridden)
to travel on a bicycle or a horse and control it as it moves
My little sister can ride a bike.

right
correct, not having any mistakes
You got all the answers right!

a b c d e f g h i j k l m n o p q **r** s t u v w x y z

a b c d e f g h i j k l m n o p q **r** s t u v w x y z

ring (rings)
1 a piece of jewellery worn on the finger
That's a pretty silver ring.
2 a circle or something that is the shape of a circle
We sat in a ring around the teacher.
3 the sound made by a bell
The phone has a loud ring.
4 a telephone call
Give me a ring tonight.

ring (ringing, rang, rung)
1 to make a sound like a bell
The doorbell rang.
2 to phone someone
Can you ring me later?

river (rivers)
a long line of water that flows to the sea
Dad is fishing by the river.

road (roads)
a track for cars, buses and lorries to travel on
The roads are very busy today.

roar (roars)
a loud noise like the sound a lion makes
There was a roar outside the tent.

robin (robins)
a small bird with a patch of red on its front
You often see robins in winter.

robot (robots)
a machine that can do things that a person can do

robots

I wish we had a robot to do the cleaning.

rock
1 the hard, stony part of the Earth's surface
We drill through rock to find oil.
2 (rocks) a large stone
We sat on the rocks by the beach.
3 a type of music that has a strong beat
My brother likes hard rock.

rocket (rockets)
1 a space vehicle shaped like a tube
The rocket is going to the moon.
2 a firework in the shape of a tube
Rockets were exploding in the sky.

rocket

roll (rolling, rolled)
to move by turning over and over
The ball rolled across the room.

roof (roofs)
the covering over the top
of a building or car
Rain leaked through the roof.

roofs

room (rooms)
part of a building that has its
own floor, walls and ceiling
There are four rooms in my house.

root (roots)
the part of a plant that is under
the ground
*Roots take water from the soil to
keep the plant alive.*

rope (ropes)
very thick string
Tie the rope tightly.

rose (roses)
a flower that grows
on a stem with thorns
The roses are blooming.

roots

rough
1 uneven, not smooth
We drove along the rough track.

2 not gentle
Don't be rough with the puppy.

**roundabout
(roundabouts)**
1 a round place where
roads meet
*Turn left at the next
roundabout.*

2 a round playground toy that
children spin and ride on
Let's ride on the roundabout.

rounders
a team game where players hit a
ball with a bat and run round the
four sides of the playing area
*We play rounders or cricket in the
summer in school.*

route (routes)
the way to go to a place
We took the quickest route home.

row (rowing, rowed)
to move a small boat
through water using oars
He rowed the boat across the lake.

royal
belonging to a queen or king
The royal coach car drove by.

a b c d e f g h i j k l m n o p q **r** s t u v w x y z

rubber

1 a strong, bouncy or stretchy material

Car tyres are made of rubber.

2 (rubbers) a small object that is used for taking pencil marks off paper

I've made a mistake in my homework. Can I use your rubber?

rubbish

1 paper and other things that are no longer needed

Put all the rubbish in the bin.

2 something that is wrong or silly

Don't talk rubbish!

ruby (rubies)

a red jewel

ruby

The queen was wearing a necklace made out of rubies and diamonds.

rude

speaking or acting in a way that is not polite

It's rude not to say 'please' and 'thank you'.

rug (rugs)

1 a small carpet

The cat is on the rug.

2 a blanket

Put the rug over your feet.

rule (rules)

a law or guide about how something must be done

It's wrong to break the rules at school.

ruler (rulers)

1 a long, flat piece of plastic or wood used to measure things or draw straight lines

I use a ruler in maths.

2 a person who has power over a country

The country didn't have a ruler when the king died.

run (running, ran, run)

1 to move your legs faster than when you are walking

Run as fast as you can!

2 to control

Mum runs her business from home.

3 to make a piece of equipment or a computer program work

Run the computer program.

run

How many things can you spot beginning with 's'?

S s

sad (sadder, saddest)
unhappy
What's happened? You look so sad.

saddle (saddles)
a seat that you sit on when you are riding a horse or a bicycle
This saddle is hard and not very comfortable.

safe (safes)
a strong box with a lock where you can keep money or jewellery
We left our money and passports in the hotel safe when we went out.

safe
not dangerous
Home is where you feel good and safe.

sail

sail (sails)
a big piece of strong material fixed to a pole on a boat, which catches the wind and makes the boat move
Let's raise the sail and go.

a b c d e f g h i j k l m n o p q r **s** t u v w x y z

a b c d e f g h i j k l m n o p q r **s** t u v w x y z

sail (sailing, sailed)
to travel across water in a boat or ship
We sailed to France on a ferry.

sailor (sailors)
someone who works on a ship
Sailors in the navy wear dark blue uniforms.

salad (salads)
vegetables or fruit mixed together, usually eaten raw
We'll put tomatoes and cucumber in the salad.

salt
very tiny grains that come from sea water and rocks, which are put on food to make it taste good
This needs a little more salt.

same
not different or changed
Look! Our clothes are exactly the same.

same

sand
tiny pieces of crushed rock
The beach is covered in beautiful, white sand.

sandal (sandals)
one of a pair of light shoes with straps that you wear in summer
I need a new pair of sandals.

Puzzle time
Can you put these sandwich instructions in the right order?
a. Next, spread one side of each slice with butter.
b. Put the cheese on one slice of bread.
c. Now put the other slice on top.
d. First, take two slices of bread.
e. Eat your sandwich

Answer: d, a, b, c, e

sandwich (sandwiches)
two pieces of bread with cheese, meat or vegetables in between
We'll make some sandwiches for the picnic.

sandwich

sari (saris)
a dress made from a long piece of thin cloth that Indian and South Asian women wear
She was wearing a blue sari.

saucer (saucers)
a small dish that goes under a cup
We put some milk in a saucer for the kitten.

sausage (sausages)
a mixture of meat, cereal and spices inside a case shaped like a tube
We had sausages and chips for dinner.

scales
a machine that is used for weighing things
Weigh the ingredients on the scales.

scar (scars)
the mark left on your skin after a cut has healed
I have a scar above my left eye.

scare (scaring, scared)
to frighten
This film will really scare you!

scarecrow (scarecrows)
an object that is made to look like a person, which is put in fields to scare off birds
We made a scarecrow out of straw.

scared
feeling afraid, frightened
Please leave a light on. I'm scared of the dark.

scarf

scarf (scarves or scarfs)
a piece of material that you wear around your neck
I'm knitting a scarf.

school (schools)
the place where children go to learn things
I started school when I was five.

science (sciences)
the study of information about the world
Biology, physics and chemistry are all types of science.

scissors
a tool for cutting things that has two sharp blades and two handles with holes for your fingers
There's a pair of scissors in the drawer.

scarecrow

a b c d e f g h i j k l m n o p q **r** **s** t u v w x y z

scooter (scooters)
1 a light motorbike with small wheels
Mum goes to work on her scooter.
2 a toy with two or three wheels and a long handle. You stand on it with one foot and use the other foot to push you along.

Riding a scooter is easier than riding a bike.

scooter

score (scores)
the number of points or goals each team or player has in a game
What's the score?

score (scoring, scored)
to get points in a game
They've scored another goal!

scorpion (scorpions)
a creature with eight legs, a curved tail and a poisonous sting
Scorpions live in warm and hot countries.

scratch (scratching, scratched)
to rub or damage your skin with your nails or something hard
Don't scratch your face.

scratch

scream (screaming, screamed)
to make a loud noise when you are afraid, angry or hurt
The swimmers screamed when they saw the shark.

screen (screens)
a flat surface on a computer or television, or in the cinema that has words or pictures on
You're sitting too close to the screen.

scribble (scribbling, scribbled)
to write or draw quickly and untidily
The baby's scribbled all over my homework.

sea
a large area of salty water
Look! You can see the sea from here.

scorpion

seal (seals)
1 a creature that lives in the sea and eats fish
Seals are good swimmers and can dive underwater for a long time.
2 wax, plastic or paper that you break to open a container
Do not buy this product if the seal is broken.

Seal

season (seasons)
the four parts of the year – spring, summer, autumn and winter
The weather is different in each season.

seaweed
a plant or plants that grow in or near to the sea
There was lots of seaweed floating in the water.

Seasons

secret
if something is secret only a few people are allowed to know about it
There's a secret passage in the house.

see (seeing, saw, seen)
1 to use your eyes to look, to watch
Did you see that programme on TV last night?
2 to understand
I've explained it to you. Now do you see?
3 to meet or visit someone
We went to see Chloe in hospital.

seed (seeds)
a small part of a plant that a new plant grows from
Put the seeds in the ground.

secret (secrets)
something that you do not want other people to know
Please don't tell anyone else – it's a secret.

seesaw (seesaws)
a long board that is balanced in the middle so that the ends go up and down
There's a seesaw in the playground.

a b c d e f g h i j k l m n o p q r **s** t u v w x y z

a b c d e f g h i j k l m n o p q r **s** t u v w x y z

send (sending, sent)
to make something go or be taken to another place
I sent her an email yesterday.

several
some, quite a few
I've seen that film several times.

sew (sewing, sewed, sewn)
to join cloth together with a needle and thread
I'll sew the button on for you.

shade
1 where the sun is not shining
Sit in the shade of the umbrella.
2 (shades) a thing to block out light
Can you pull the shade down, please?
3 (shades) a colour
That's a nice shade of green.

shadow (shadows)
a dark shape that appears on the ground when something is blocking the light
You can see your shadow on a sunny day.

shake (shaking, shook, shaken)
to move something quickly up and down or side to side
Shake the bottle well before opening.

shampoo (shampoos)
liquid soap for washing your hair
Did you bring the shampoo?

shape (shapes)
the outline or form of a thing
What shape is it?

shapes

shark (sharks)
a large fish that usually has sharp teeth
Some sharks can be dangerous to humans.

sheep (plural is the same)
a farm animal kept for wool and meat
There are sheep on the hill.

shadow

shelf (shelves)
a board, usually wooden, fixed on a wall for putting things on
Can you reach that shelf?

shell (shells)
the hard covering of an egg, a seed or an animal such as a turtle or a crab
Ostrich eggs are very big and have thick shells.

ship (ships)
a large boat
The ship sailed across the ocean.

shirt (shirts)
a piece of clothing with buttons that you wear on the top half of your body
Tuck your shirt in.

shiver (shivering, shivered)
to shake because you are cold or scared
You're shivering! Put on your fleece.

shivering

shock (shocks)
1 a bad surprise
The bill was quite a shock.

2 a pain you feel when electricity goes through your body
I got a shock from that plug!

shoe (shoes)
one of two coverings for your feet that are usually made of strong material
Mum's wardrobe is full of shoes.

shoes

shoot (shooting, shot)
1 to fire a gun
Don't shoot!
2 to kick or throw a ball into a goal or net in a game
Shoot when you are closer to the basket.

shop (shops)
a place that sells things
What time does the shop open?

short
1 not tall
My brother is shorter than me.
2 not long
My sister has short hair.
3 not lasting a long time
Let's take a short break.

a b c d e f g h i j k l m n o p q r **s** t u v w x y z

a b c d e f g h i j k l m n o p q r **s** t u v w x y z

shorts
short trousers
We wear shorts in summer.

shoulder (shoulders)
the top of your arm where it joins your body
Put the bag over your shoulder.

shout (shouting, shouted)
to call out to someone in a loud voice
There's no need to shout at me; I'm right here!

shout

show (showing, showed, shown)
1 to let someone see something
Show me your new game.
2 to guide someone somewhere or help them to do something
The guide showed us around.

shower (showers)
1 something that you stand under to wash your body
Every room in the hotel has a private shower.
2 a light fall of rain
There will be showers in the afternoon.

shrink (shrinking, shrank, shrunk)
to become smaller
My favourite jumper shrank in the wash.

shut (shutting, shut)
to close
Shut the door, please.

sideways
towards one side, not forwards or backwards
Turn sideways and then you can get past.

sign (signs)
1 a mark or symbol that means something
The sign £ means pound or pounds.
2 a notice that tells you something
The sign says 'Danger of avalanche'.

sign (signing, signed)
to write your name on something
Sign your name at the bottom of the form.

sign

silly (sillier, silliest)
stupid, not sensible
Don't be so silly!

similar
nearly the same as something else
My brother and I look similar and we like similar things.

sing (singing, sang, sung)
to make music with your voice
Sing us a song.

sink (sinks)
a bowl with taps in a kitchen or a bathroom
Put the dirty dishes in the sink.

sink

sink (sinking, sank, sunk)
to go down below the surface of water
The ship Titanic sank after it hit an iceberg.

sister (sisters)
a girl or woman who has the same parents as you
Shannon is my younger sister.

sit (sitting, sat)
to put your bottom on a chair or another type of seat
I must sit down; my feet ache.

size (sizes)
how big or small something is
These shoes come in all sizes.

skate (skates)
a boot with wheels or a blade fixed to the bottom
We're going to the park. Don't forget your skates.

skate (skating, skated)
to move over ground or ice wearing boots with wheels or blades
He skated over to us when he saw us.

skateboard (skateboards)
a small board on wheels that you can ride on
He came down the ramp on his skateboard.

skateboard

a b c d e f g h i j k l m n o p q r **s** t u v w x y z

skeleton (skeletons)
the bones in your body
He wore a suit with a skeleton painted on it for Hallowe'en.

skeleton

sketch (sketching, sketched)
to draw quickly
Artists sketch a scene first.

ski (skis)
a long, flat piece of wood or plastic that you fix to special shoes for moving along on snow
We carried our skis to the top of the mountain.

ski (skiing, skied)
to move quickly over snow or water on long, narrow pieces of wood
Do you know how to ski?

skin (skins)
the outside layer covering your body, or covering fruits and vegetables
The skin is the body's largest organ.

skirt (skirts)
a piece of clothing worn by girls and women that hangs from the waist down
She was wearing a blue skirt and red jacket.

sky (skies)
the space above you where the sun, moon, stars and clouds are
The sky was full of stars.

slap (slapping, slapped)
to hit something with an open hand
She slapped his hand.

sledge (sledges)
a vehicle or toy for moving across ice or snow
We built a sledge out of an old wooden box.

sleep (sleeping, slept)
not to be awake
The baby is sleeping.

sleeping

slice (slices)
a thin piece of bread, cake, meat or other food that has been cut from a bigger piece
Can you eat another slice of meat?

slices

slide (slides)
1 a structure with steps and a slope that you climb then slide smoothly down
My favourite thing in the playground is the slide.
2 a small piece of metal or plastic that girls wear in their hair to keep it away from their face
My slide is shaped like a butterfly.

slide (sliding, slid)
to move across or down a smooth surface
The car slid across the ice.

slipper (slippers)
one of a pair of soft shoes that you wear indoors
Put your slippers on if your feet are cold.

slow
not fast, taking a long time
This is a slow train.

small
little or young
The jeans have a small pocket for coins.

smile (smiling, smiled)
to make your mouth curve up and look happy
The photographer asked us to smile.

smoke
the cloudy gas that is made when something burns
The room filled with smoke.

smooth
not rough or bumpy
You can skate on the pavement; it's smooth.

smoke

snack (snacks)
a small meal that you can prepare quickly
Let's just have a snack now because we're having a big meal this evening.

snail (snails)
a small creature with a soft, wet body and a shell on its back
Snails move very slowly.

snail

a b c d e f g h i j k l m n o p q r **s** t u v w x y z

snake (snakes)
a creature with a long body and no legs
I hope there aren't any snakes in the grass.

s**nake**

sneeze (sneezing, sneezed)
to blow air out of your nose suddenly, with a loud noise
He's sneezing and coughing because he has a cold.

snow
small, soft pieces of ice that fall from the sky
The trees are covered in snow.

snow (snowing, snowed)
when it snows, small soft pieces of ice fall from the sky
Hurrah! It's snowing. Let's build a snowman.

snowing

soap
something that you use with water to wash your body
The soap is making lots of bubbles.

soccer
football, a game played by two teams that try to get a round ball between two posts
Do you prefer soccer or cricket?

sock (socks)
one of two pieces of clothing that you wear on your feet
Socks keep your feet warm.

sofa (sofas)
a long, soft seat for two or more people
Shall we sit on the sofa?

soft
1 not hard, smooth when you touch it
  The rabbit has lovely, soft fur.
2 not loud
  She has a soft voice.

software
the programs that run on a computer
He designs software.

soldier (soldiers)
a person in the army
The soldiers marched through the square.

soldier

solid
hard, firm
The front door is made of solid wood.

some
1 an amount of something that is not exact
Would you like some rice?
2 part of something, but not all
Some of these apples are rotten.

son (sons)
a male child
They have two sons.

song (songs)
a piece of music with words
The children sang songs in the school hall.

Space

sore
hurting or painful
Is the cut on your leg still sore?

sorry
feeling sad because something bad or unpleasant has happened
I'm sorry your mum is ill.

soup
a liquid food made from meat or vegetables and water
Have a bowl of tomato soup.

sour
having a taste like lemons, not sweet
This juice is a bit sour.

space
1 (spaces) an empty or open place
Is there any space left in the suitcase?
2 everything beyond the Earth's air
The rocket is travelling through space.

spade (spades)
a tool for digging
Turn the soil with a spade.

spaghetti
long, thin strips of pasta
Ellie likes spaghetti.

Spaghetti

spare
extra, not needed at the moment
I've got a spare pencil if you need one.

a b c d e f g h i j k l m n o p q r s t u v w x y z

a b c d e f g h i j k l m n o p q r **s** t u v w x y z

speed (speeds)
how fast something moves
At what speed are we travelling?

spell (spelling, spelt, spelled)
to write or say the letters of a
word in the correct order
How do you spell 'skateboard'?

Spider

spider (spiders)
a small creature
with eight legs
that catches insects in a web
There's a spider in the bath.

spill (spilling, spilt, spilled)
to cause a liquid to fall to the
ground accidentally
I spilt the drink on the carpet.

spilt

Puzzle time
Can you unscramble the
names of these sports?

a. gruyb b. gsmwmin
c. cykeoh d. nintes

Answers: a. rugby
b. swimming c. hockey
d. tennis

spoon (spoons)
an object with a handle and
small bowl that is used
for eating
*We need knives,
forks and spoons
on the table.*

sport

sport
physical
activities such as
swimming and soccer
*Swimming is a sport the
whole family can enjoy.*

spring
the time of year
between winter and summer
The cherry tree flowers in spring.

squirrel (squirrels)
a small wild animal with a long,
bushy tail
*Squirrels are very good at climbing
trees.*

stadium (stadiums)
a big building where you can
watch sports matches or concerts
*Some stadiums have roofs and
some don't.*

stairs
a set of steps in a building that go from one floor to another
I'll take the stairs to the top floor.

stamp (stamps)
1 a piece of paper that you stick on a letter or postcard before you post it
I'd like a first class stamp.
2 a tool you put ink on and then press onto something to make a mark
There's a stamp on the library book showing the date you have to take it back.

Statue

stand (standing, stood)
to be on your feet
She's standing by the door.

star (stars)
1 a ball of burning gas that looks like a light in the sky
The stars are bright tonight
2 a famous person
She's a big star now.
3 a shape with five or six points
We baked biscuits shaped like stars.

starfish (starfish or starfishes)
a star-shaped creature that lives in the sea
There's a starfish under the rock.

start (starting, started)
to begin
We started work at 10 o'clock this morning.

station (stations)
a place where trains and buses stop to let people on and off
My dad walks to the station every morning then gets the train.

statue (statues)
a model of a person or animal made out of stone or metal
There's a statue of a mermaid in the middle of the fountain.

stay (staying, stayed)
1 not to leave a place
You stay here; I'll be right back.
2 to live in a place for a short amount of time
When I was little, we stayed at my aunt's house every summer.
3 to continue to remain the same
He's never grumpy, his mood stays the same all the time.

a b c d e f g h i j k l m n o p q r **s** t u v w x y z

steal (stealing, stole, stolen)
to take something that doesn't belong to you
Thieves stole my dad's car.

steam

steam
the hot gas that comes off boiling water
The kitchen is full of steam because I forgot to put the lid on the kettle.

stick (sticks)
a long, thin piece of wood
We made a fire by rubbing two sticks together.

stomach (stomachs)
the part inside your body where food goes when you eat
My stomach hurts; I've eaten too much.

stone
1 the hard solid substance found in the ground, rock
The floor in the castle is made out of stone.
2 (stones) fourteen pounds or 6.35 kilograms
What is your weight in stones?

3 (stones) the seed in some fruits
Careful! The cherries have stones in them.

stool (stools)
a seat with no back
Sit on the stool.

stop (stopping, stopped)
1 to finish doing something
Stop talking for a minute.
2 not to move any more
You have to stop if the traffic lights are red.
3 to prevent something happening
The referee stopped the fight.

storm (storms)
a time of very bad weather with heavy rain, wind and sometimes thunder and lightning
A lot of trees fell down in the storm.

storm

story (stories)
a description of events that may be real or imaginary
Everyone knows the story of Peter Pan.

straight

not crooked, bent or curly

She has straight hair.

strange

1 unusual

He looks a bit strange.

2 unfamiliar

There were a lot of strange faces at the party.

stranger (strangers)

someone you don't know

You must never get into a stranger's car.

strawberries

strawberry (strawberries)

a soft, heart-shaped, red fruit

We sometimes have strawberries and cream in summer.

stream (streams)

a small river

We drank water from a mountain stream.

stretch (stretching, stretched)

1 to get longer or bigger

Tights can stretch quite a bit.

2 to straighten a part of your body

She stretched her legs out under the table.

string

thick thread or thin rope

Tie some string around the box.

strong

1 powerful, not weak

She must be very strong if she can carry this suitcase.

2 not easily broken or damaged

The window is made from very strong glass.

stupid

not sensible or clever

What a stupid idea!

submarine (submarines)

a ship that can travel underwater

Submarines can help us to find out about underwater life.

sudden

happening quickly and unexpectedly

Don't make any sudden movements.

submarine

a b c d e f g h i j k l m n o p q r **s** t u v w x y z

a b c d e f g h i j k l m n o p q r **s** t u v w x y z

sugar
a sweet substance used to
flavour food
Sugar can be white or brown.

suitcase (suitcases)
a case or bag to carry
clothes in when you travel
Our suitcase has wheels.

summer (summers)
the time of year
between spring and autumn
*Are you going on holiday this
summer?*

sun (Sun)
the very bright star that the
Earth travels around
*All the planets in the solar system
travel around the Sun.*

sunflower (sunflowers)
a tall flower whose head is round
and yellow like the sun
*Sunflowers look
like big,
yellow
daisies.*

sunflowers

sunglasses
dark glasses that you wear to
protect your eyes when it is sunny
Don't forget to pack your sunglasses.

suitcases

**supermarket
(supermarkets)**
a large shop that
sells food and other
things
*The supermarket
stays open late on
Fridays.*

supper (suppers)
a meal you eat in the evening,
or a snack you eat just before
bedtime
*For supper I usually have tea and
toast.*

surprise (surprises)
something that is completely
unexpected
*A bunch of flowers! What a lovely
surprise!*

swan (swans)
a white bird with a long neck that
lives on rivers and lakes
*Swans glide smoothly across the
water.*

sweep (sweeping, swept)
to brush dirt from the floor or ground
Have you swept the floor?

sweet (sweets)
1 a small piece of sweet, sugary food such as a chocolate or toffee
Always clean your teeth after eating sweets.
2 a pudding or dessert
For sweet we could have strawberries and ice cream.

sweet
1 tasting sugary
These grapes are very sweet.
2 nice or pleasant
That's a sweet thing to say.

swim (swimming, swam, swum)
to move through or across water by using your arms and legs
I can swim a whole length of the pool.

swim

s w o r d

swimming pool (swimming pools)
a big, deep hole that contains water, where you can swim
There's an outdoor swimming pool in this town.

swing (swings)
a seat hanging from a bar or a tree that moves backwards and forwards
I'll sit on the swing first and you can push me.

swing (swinging, swung)
to move backwards, forwards or from side to side from a fixed point
The monkey swung from tree to tree.

sword (swords)
a very large knife that was used for fighting in the past
There are lots of old swords in the museum.

synagogue (synagogues)
a building where Jewish people go to pray
My uncle got married in a synagogue.

a b c d e f g h i j k l m n o p q r **s** t u v w x y z

How many things can you spot beginning with 't'?

T t

table (tables)
1 a piece of furniture with legs and a flat top
Please clear the table.
2 a list of numbers or words written in rows and columns
We measured the height of everyone in the class and wrote the results in a table.

tadpole (tadpoles)
a very young frog or toad
Tadpoles have big heads and long tails and live in water.

tail (tails)
the part of an animal at the end of its back
The dog has a long, white tail.

— tail

take (taking, took, taken)
1 to carry something
Take an umbrella with you.
2 to move something or someone to another place
Can you take us to the station?
3 to steal
The thieves took all the money.

talent (talents)
the ability to do something very well without having to learn it
Maya has a talent for drawing.

talk (talking, talked)
to speak
We talked on the phone for ages.

tall
1 higher than normal
My grandad is tall, and I am short.
2 having a certain height
How tall are you?

tambourine (tambourines)
a small round musical instrument that you shake or hit
I played the tambourine in the school concert.

tank (tanks)
1 a container for liquids
There's a leak in the petrol tank.
2 a strong truck used by soldiers
Tanks have metal tracks or belts instead of wheels.

tap (taps)
something that controls the flow of a liquid or gas
Turn the tap off; don't waste water.

tape
a flat, narrow strip of plastic that is sticky on one side
Put some sticky tape on the envelope.

taste (tasting, tasted)
1 to have a flavour
What does the soup taste like?
2 to try a little food or drink to see what it is like
Have you tasted the pizza?

taxi (taxis)
a car that takes people to different places, for money
We'll take a taxi.

tea
1 a hot drink made from leaves
Do you take milk in your tea?
2 a meal you eat in the early evening
What's for tea?

teacher (teachers)

a person who gives lessons in a subject
Our teacher's name is Mrs Griffiths.

teacher

team (teams)
a group of people
who play a game or
work together
*There are eleven
players in a football
team.*

**tear (tears)
(rhymes with ear)**
a drop of water that
comes out of your eye
Tears ran down his face.

**tear (tearing, tore,
torn) (rhymes with fair)**
to rip, split or make a hole in
something
I tore the paper in half.

teddy bear (teddy bears)
a soft toy that looks like a bear
*I take my teddy bear to
bed with me.*

telephone (telephones)
a piece of equipment
that you use to speak to
someone in another place
Where's your telephone?

Puzzle time
Can you match these star
patterns to the names below?
1. Pegasus (the winged horse)
2. Ursa Major (Great Bear)
3. Hercules
4. Orion (the Hunter)

a

b

c

d

Answers: 1d 2b 3a 4c

**telescope
(telescopes)**
a piece of
equipment that
you use to look
at things that are
far away
*We looked at the
stars through the
telescope.*

**television (TV;
televisions)**
a machine with
a screen that shows programmes
*What's on television tomorrow
evening?*

tell (telling, told)
1 to pass on information
I told you that story yesterday.
2 to know or understand
I can't tell what it means.

temple (temples)
a building where
people of some
religions go to pray
*Hindus and
Buddhists
worship in a
temple.*

teddy bear

tennis

tennis
a game played by two or four people who hit a ball over a net to score points
Tennis is a summer game.

tent (tents)
a temporary shelter made of cloth or plastic
The tent will keep us dry.

terrible
very bad
The film was terrible.

tent

test (tests)
1 a set of questions to measure knowledge
We had a spelling test at school today.

2 a set of checks to find out if something is working properly
Cars must pass several tests.

text (texts)
1 a message you send by mobile phone
Send me a text when you are on the train.
2 the writing in a book or magazine, not the pictures
The book has fifty pages of text.

text (texting, texted)
to send someone a message by mobile phone
I'll text you later.

thank (thanking, thanked)
to tell someone you are pleased about something they have given you or have done for you
Remember to thank them for the present.

theatre (theatres)
a building where you can go and see plays
Shall we go to the theatre this weekend?

a b c d e f g h i j k l m n o p q r s **t** u v w x y z

a b c d e f g h i j k l m n o p q r s **t** u v w x y z

thick
1 not thin
The furniture was covered with a thick sheet of plastic.
2 not watery
This pancake mixture is too thick.

thief (thieves)
a person who steals things
The police chased the thief.

thin (thinner, thinnest)
1 having not much distance from one side to the other
Cut the paper into thin strips.
2 slim, not fat
She's quite thin.
3 watery
It's a thin, clear soup.

think (thinking, thought)
1 to use your mind to solve a problem or remember something
Think carefully before you answer.
2 to believe something is true, but not to know for sure
I think we break up next Wednesday.

thirsty (thirstier, thirstiest)
feeling that you need to drink something
Are you thirsty?

throw

throat (throats)
the back of your mouth where food goes when you swallow
I've got a bone stuck in my throat.

through
from one side to the other
The cat came in through the cat flap.

throw (throwing, threw, thrown)
to make something go through the air
Throw the ball through the net.

thumb (thumbs)
the short, thick finger on the inside of your hand
I've cut my thumb.

thunder
the loud noise you can hear during a storm
There was thunder and lightning.

ticket (tickets)
a piece of paper that shows you have paid
I have tickets for the match on Saturday.

tickets

tidy (tidier, tidiest)
neat and organized
Leah's room is never tidy.

tie (ties)
a long strip of material that you wear under a shirt collar and tie at the front
We have to wear ties in our school.

tie (tying, tied)
to join pieces of string, rope or thread together
Tie your shoelaces.

tiger (tigers)
a large, wild cat with orange fur with black stripes
Tigers live in India and Southeast Asia.

tiger

tight
1 close-fitting
This shirt is a bit tight.
2 firmly in place
I can't undo the knot; it's too tight.

tights
clothing worn by girls and women on the feet and legs
I always wear thick tights in winter.

timetable (timetables)
a list of times when things happen or buses and trains leave
Check the timetable to see when the next train is.

tiny (tinier, tiniest)
very small
Look at the tiny ladybird.

tired
feeling that you need to rest
The baby is tired.

toad (toads)
a creature like a big frog
Toads have drier skin than frogs.

toast
bread that has been cooked in a toaster or under a grill
I have toast and marmalade for breakfast.

today
this day
What's the date today?

toe (toes)
one of the five parts of your body at the end of your foot
Ouch! You stood on my toe.

toes

together

1 joined or mixed

Mix the eggs and milk together.

2 with each other

Shall we go together?

tomatoes

tomato (tomatoes)

a red fruit that you
can eat raw or cooked

Mum sliced a tomato for the salad.

tomorrow

the day after today

What shall we do tomorrow?

tool (tools)

a piece of equipment that you
use to do a job

Hammers and saws are tools.

tongue (tongues)

the part of your body inside your
mouth that you use to speak with
and to taste things

I can curl my tongue.

tooth (teeth)

one of the hard, white
things in your mouth

*You should brush your
teeth twice a day.*

top (tops)

1 the highest part of something

*They reached the top of the
    mountain.*

2 a piece of clothing for
the upper body

That's a pretty top.

3 a cover or lid for a
container

Put the top back on the bottle.

4 a toy that spins round

The top is brightly coloured.

torch (torches)

a light that you can carry around
with you

Shine the torch over here.

tortoise (tortoises)

a small animal with a thick, hard
shell that it can pull its legs and
head into

Tortoises move very slowly.

touch (touching, touched)

1 to put
your fingers
or hand on
something

*Please don't
touch the
paintings.*

teeth

2 to be so close to another thing that there is no space between the two
The wires are touching.

towel (towels)
a cloth that you use to dry things that are wet
Dry your hands on the towel.

tower

tower (towers)
a tall, narrow building or part of a building
We climbed to the top of the tower.

town (towns)
a place with houses and other buildings where people live and work
There's a theatre in our town.

toy (toys)
something that children like to play with
The baby has lots of toys.

toys

tractor (tractors)
a big truck that farm workers drive
We were behind a tractor on the road so we had to drive slowly.

traffic
all the cars, buses, lorries and other vehicles that are travelling on a road
The traffic on this road is very heavy.

traffic jam (traffic jams)
a line of traffic that is moving very slowly or is not moving at all
We were stuck in a traffic jam for nearly an hour.

traffic lights
a set of red, orange and green lights where two or more roads meet
Turn left at the traffic lights.

train (trains)
a line of carriages pulled by an engine on a track
Mum goes to work on the train.

trainer (trainers)
a sports shoe
I bought some new trainers.

trampoline (trampolines)
a large piece of stretchy cloth attached to a metal frame that you can bounce up and down on
We all had a go on the trampoline.

a b c d e f g h i j k l m n o p q r s **t** u v w x y z

transport (transporting, transported)
to move people or things from one place to another
The tanker transports petrol.

trap (trapping, trapped)
to catch something in a piece of equipment
It traps mice.

trapeze (trapezes)
a bar hanging from two ropes that people swing from
I liked the acrobats on the trapeze best when we went to the circus.

travel (travelling, travelled)
to go from one place to another
They're travelling by car.

treasure
valuable things like gold or jewellery
The chest is filled with treasure.

tree (trees)
a large, tall plant with a trunk and branches
There's a big tree in our garden.

trick (tricks)
1 something clever that you do
The magician knows lots of tricks.
2 something that people do to fool or cheat someone
He played a mean trick on me.

trip (trips)
a journey
We've decided to go on a trip around the world.

trip (tripping, tripped)
to catch your foot on something and nearly fall
I tripped as I was coming down the steps.

trousers
a piece of clothing that covers the legs
He's wearing grey trousers.

truck (trucks)
a lorry
We were stuck behind a truck.

trunk (trunks)
1 the thick part of a tree
I sat on the grass with my back against the trunk of the tree.

tree

trunk

2 an elephant's nose
The elephant has a long trunk.
3 a box for storing things in
Where's the key for this trunk?

try (trying, tried)
1 to make an effort
I tried to open the window.
2 to test or sample something
Have you tried this cake?

**T-shirt/t-shirt
(T-shirts)**
a piece of clothing
like a vest with short
sleeves
*I love my purple
T-shirt.*

T-shirt

tunnel (tunnels)
a long hole under the ground
*There is a tunnel under the sea
between England and France.*

turkey
1 (turkeys) a large bird that is
kept on farms for its meat
*There are hundreds of turkeys on
the farm.*
2 the meat from this bird
*We usually have turkey for
Christmas dinner.*

turn (turns)
your time to play or to do
something, your go in a game
Is it my turn yet?

turn (turning, turned)
1 to move so you are looking or
going in a new direction
Turn round and face the door.
2 to move something to a
different position
Turn the key.

turtle (turtles)
an animal that lives in water
that looks like a tortoise
*Turtles have thick shells
covering their bodies.*

twin (twins)
your brother or
sister born at
the same time
as you
*Tom and Dylan
are twins.*

twins

tyre (tyres)
a rubber ring that goes around
the wheel of a car or bicycle
I think one of the tyres is flat.

How many things can you spot beginning with 'u'?

Uu

ugly (uglier, ugliest)
not nice to look at
What an ugly colour!

umbrella (umbrellas)
a piece of material stretched
over a frame with a handle, that
keeps the rain off
*It's raining
outside; I'll
take my
umbrella.*

umbrella

uncle (uncles)
the brother of your mother or
father, or the husband of your
aunt
*He looks like
his uncle.*

under
below
Put your bag   under
under your seat.

**understand (understanding,
understood)**
1 to know the meaning of words
or ideas
Does he understand English?
2 to know how something works
*I don't understand how the
machine works.*

3 to know how and why someone feels or acts a certain way
You don't understand.

underwear
pieces of clothing that you wear next to your body, under your other clothes
Vests and pants are items of underwear.

unhappy (unhappier, unhappiest)
not happy, sad
Cheer up! Try not to look so unhappy.

unicorn

unicorn (unicorns)
an animal in stories that looks like a white horse with a horn growing out of the front of its head
In the story, the prince searched for the unicorn in the forest.

uniform (uniforms)
a set of clothes worn by everyone in a group of people
In school we wear a uniform.

universe (universes)
all the planets, all the stars, the Sun and everything in space
Is there life anywhere else in the universe?

up
towards a higher position
Pass that brush up to me.

upset
1 feeling sad or worried
She was upset to hear the bad news.
2 feeling bad or sick
He's got an upset stomach.

upside-down

upside-down
turned over so that the top is at the bottom and the bottom is at the top
Turn the bottle upside-down and the sauce will come out.

upstairs
towards or on a higher floor of a building
I went upstairs to my bedroom.

urgent
needing attention immediately
Tell the headmistress it's urgent.

a b c d e f g h i j k l m n o p q r s t **u** v w x y z

a b c d e f g h i j k l m n o p q r s t u v w x y z

How many things can you spot beginning with 'v'?

V v

vanish (vanishing, vanished)
to disappear
The deer suddenly vanished.

vase (vases)
a container to put flowers in
Mum put the roses in a vase.

valley (valleys)
the low land between
two hills
There is a river in the valley.

vegetable (vegetables)
a plant grown for food
Carrots are my favourite vegetable.

vegetarian (vegetarians)
a person who doesn't eat meat
My best friend is a vegetarian.

van (vans)
a boxlike vehicle that
is bigger than a car
but smaller than a
lorry
*The plumber arrived
in a van.*

vehicle (vehicles)
a machine that moves people or
things from one place to another
Cars and trucks are vehicles.

vase

vest (vests)
a piece of clothing that you wear on your upper body under your other clothes
Put a vest on; it's cold today.

vet (veterinary surgeon; vets)
an animal doctor
The vet is treating our dog.

view (views)
everything you can see from a place
There's a lovely view from this window.

village (villages)
a group of houses and buildings in the country
It's a beautiful, old village.

vinegar
a sour liquid used to keep food fresh, or to give it a sharp taste
I like vinegar on chips.

violin

violin (violins)
a musical instrument that you hold under your chin and play with a bow
My brother is learning to play the violin.

virus (viruses)
1 a very tiny living thing that can make you ill if it gets inside your body
Flu is caused by a virus.
2 a computer program that damages information stored on a computer
The virus has damaged my files.

visit (visiting, visited)
to go to see a person or a place
We visit my grandparents every Sunday.

voice (voices)
the sound you make when you are speaking or singing
I didn't recognize your voice.

volcano (volcanoes)
a mountain with an opening that sprays out lava and ash
Mount Etna in Italy is an active volcano.

volcano

vote (voting, voted)
to show which idea or person you choose by raising your hand or writing on paper
Let's vote on this idea.

a b c d e f g h i j k l m n o p q r s t u **v** w x y z

How many things can you spot beginning with 'w'?

W w

waiter (waiters)
a man who serves food in a
restaurant or café
*The waiter gave each
of us a menu.*

waitress (waitresses)
a woman who serves
food in a restaurant
or café
*Ask the waitress
for the bill.*

waitress

wake (waking, woke, woken)
to stop sleeping
I woke up at eight o'clock.

walk (walking, walked)
to move along, putting one foot
in front of the other
I walk to school every day.

walk

wall (walls)
1 the side of a room or a building
There are some pictures on the wall.
2 a structure made of stone
or bricks that goes around a
garden or field
We climbed over the wall.

wand (wands)
a special stick used by fairies, witches and magicians to do magic
With a flick of her wand she turned the pumpkin into a coach.

wand

want (wanting, wanted)
if you want something you would like to have it or do it
Do you want a sandwich?

wardrobe (wardrobes)
a cupboard to hang clothes in
I have a wardrobe in my bedroom.

warm
slightly hot, not cool or cold
The water is lovely and warm.

wash (washing, washed)
to clean with water
I washed my hands.

wasp (wasps)
a black-and-yellow flying insect that stings
wasp
Wasps live in nests.

watch (watches)
a small clock that you wear on your wrist
I'd like a watch for my birthday.

watch (watching, watched)
to look at something and pay attention
We're watching the match.

water
a liquid that falls from the sky as rain
There is water in rivers and lakes.

waterfall (waterfalls)
water from a stream or a river that falls straight down over rocks
There is a pool under the waterfall.

wave (waves)
1 a raised part of moving water on the sea
Waves crashed on the beach.
2 a movement of your hand from side to side to say hello or goodbye
Give them a wave.
3 the way light and sound move
Sound is carried on radio waves.

wave (waving, waved)

1 to move your hand from side to side to say hello or goodbye
She waved to me from the other side of the road.
2 to move from side to side
The children waved their flags.

wave

weak

not strong
I feel weak and dizzy.

wear (wearing, wore, worn)

to have clothes on your body
What shall I wear to the party?

weather

the condition of the air – how hot it is, the wind, rain and clouds
What's the weather like today?

web

1 (webs) the very thin net a spider weaves
Spiders catch food in webs.
2 the World Wide Web on the Internet
You'll find the information on the web.

website (websites)

a place on the Internet where you can find out things
Please visit our website.

weed (weeds)

a plant that grows in a place where you do not want it to be
There are lots of weeds in our garden.

week (weeks)

seven days
We went to Spain for two weeks.

weekend (weekends)

Saturday and Sunday
We're going away for the weekend.

weigh (weighing, weighed)

1 to measure how heavy something is
The shop assistant weighed the fruit.
2 to be heavy or light
How much do you weigh?

weigh

well (wells)

a deep hole in the ground with water or oil at the bottom
People used to get water from wells.

well

1 in a good way

You played that tune very well.

2 healthy, not ill

Get well soon.

wet (wetter, wettest)

covered in water

Your hair's still wet.

whales

whale (whales)

a very large sea animal

Whales are mammals, not fish.

wheat

a cereal plant that is used to make flour

These fields are used to grow wheat.

wheel (wheels)

a round object that turns and moves a vehicle along

The wheel came off my bike.

whisker (whiskers)

one of the long, stiff hairs on an animal's face

My cat has long whiskers.

whisper (whispering, whispered)

to speak very quietly

Whisper the secret to me.

whistle (whistles)

a thing you blow into to make a loud, high sound

The referee blew his whistle.

whistle

whistle (whistling, whistled)

to blow air out through your lips and make a sound

Can you whistle?

wicked

very bad or evil

The wicked witch trapped them.

wife (wives)

A woman who is married

His wife is very nice.

win (winning, won)

to be the first or the best in a race or other competition

He's won the race!

wind (winds)

air moving across the ground

There's a strong wind today.

a b c d e f g h i j k l m n o p q r s t u v **w** x y z

a b c d e f g h i j k l m n o p q r s t u v **w** x y z

windmill (windmills)
a building with long blades, called sails, that turn in the wind
Windmills were used to generate electricity.

window (windows)
an opening in a wall that is covered by glass
She looked out of the window.

wing (wings)
1 one of the parts of a bird's or insect's body that it uses for flying
The bird flapped its wings.
2 one of the flat parts of an aeroplane that sticks out at the side and helps the plane move through the air
I sat over the wing when I flew in a plane.

winter (winters)
the time of year between autumn and spring
The weather is colder in winter.

wish (wishes)
a feeling of wanting something very much
The fairy gave me three wishes.

wish (wishing, wished)
to hope for or want something
What did you wish for?

witch (witches)
a woman in stories who has magic powers
The witch rode on a broomstick.

wizard

wizard (wizards)
a man in stories who has magic powers
The wizard broke the spell.

wolf (wolves)
a wild animal that looks like a large dog
Wolves hunt in packs, or groups.

wolf

woman (women)
a female adult
Are there any women in the team?

wonder (wondering, wondered)
to think about something and why it is that way
I wonder why she said that?

wood

1 the hard material that a tree is made of
Put more wood on the fire.
2 (woods) an area of land where a lot of trees grow
We walked through the wood.

wool

wool

thick, soft hair that grows on sheep's bodies and that can be made into thread
I need four balls of wool to knit a scarf.

work (working, worked)

1 to do a job
She works in the hospital as a doctor.
2 to go or operate smoothly
This machine is working properly now.

world

our planet and everything that is on it
There are over six billion people in the world.

worm (worms)

a long, thin creature with no legs that lives in soil
Worms are good for the garden.

worry (worrying, worried)

to have the feeling that something bad might happen
Don't worry; I'll be all right.

worse (worst)

less good
My cold is worse today.

Puzzle time

Match the workers with the things they need to do their jobs

A	B
actor	paint
artist	theatre
pilot	menu
waiter	plane

Answers: actor/theatre
artist/paint pilot/plane
waiter/menu

wrist (wrists)

the place where your arm and hand are joined
She was wearing a bracelet on her wrist.

write (writing, wrote, written)

to put words on paper using a pen or pencil
I wrote her a letter.

wrong

not right, incorrect
We've taken a wrong turn.

a b c d e f g h i j k l m n o p q r s t u v **w** x y z

a b c d e f g h i j k l m n o p q r s t u v w x y z

How many things can you spot beginning with 'x', 'y' and 'z'?

xyz

X-ray (X-rays)
1 a beam of energy that can go through solid things
X-rays are used at airports.
2 a photograph of the inside of the body
The X-ray shows that his hand may be broken.

xylophone (xylophones)
a musical instrument that you play by hitting wooden or metal bars with sticks
My baby sister has a toy xylophone.

yacht (yachts)
a sailing boat
They sailed around France in a yacht.

yawn (yawning, yawned)
to open your mouth and take a deep breath, usually when you are tired
You're yawning. It must be bedtime.

year (years)
a period of 12 months, especially from January to December
We've lived here for five years.

yell (yelling, yelled)
to shout very loudly
The teacher told us not to yell in the classroom.

yes

a word that you say when you agree with something or when something is true
Yes, you're right.

yesterday

the day before today
I phoned you yesterday.

yoga

exercises for your body and mind
My mum does yoga on a mat.

yoghurt (or yogurt)

a thick liquid food made from milk
I'd like a strawberry yoghurt, please.

yolk (yolks)

the yellow part of an egg
I like dipping my toast into the yolk.

young

not old, not yet an adult
You're too young to walk to school on your own.

yo-yo (yo-yos)

a toy that moves up and down on a string that you hold in your hand
This yo-yo glows in the dark.

zebra (zebras)

a wild, black-and-white striped animal
Zebras look like horses.

zebra

zebra crossing (zebra crossings)

part of a road painted with black-and-white stripes where you can cross the road safely
The driver stopped at the zebra crossing so the children could cross the road.

zero

nothing, 0
The temperature is zero degrees.

zip (zips)

a fastener made of two rows of teeth that lock together
Some of my skirts have zips and some have buttons.

zoo (zoos)

a place where wild animals are kept so that people can go to look at them
We went to the zoo.

yo-yo

a b c d e f g h i j k l m n o p q r s t u v w x y z

ACKNOWLEDGEMENTS

The publishers would like to thank the following sources for the use of their photographs:

Key t=top, b=bottom, l=left, r=right, c=centre

COVER (all Shutterstock.com): Front(tc) arosoft, (b) Robert Eastman; spine(t) Vaclav Volrab; back(cl) Bjorn Heller, (bc) Eric Isselee

Dreamstime
24(b) Elena Schweitzer; 60(br) Miroslava Holasová ; 21(b) Mike Lambert

Fotolia
15 Andrew Bruce; 17 Tomasz Trojanowski; 29(r) NiDerLander; 30(b) Maksim Shebeko; 41(b); 42; 48(b) Maksim Shebeko; 58(cl); 68; 84(t) Alx; 92 Fatman73; 103(tr) Oleg Belyakov; 118(c); 134(r) Sweet Angel; 136(t) Joe Gough; 138(t) klikk; 143(b); 155(b) ivan kmit; 180(bl) Phimak; 180(cr) Eric Isselée

iStock
23(t) DNY59; 30(t) 3060917; 39 coloroftime; 48(t) janrysavy; 52 Seb Chandler; 71(b) P_Wei; 81(t) Elena Kalistratova; 89(tr) Tony Campbell; 114(b) Skeezer

Shutterstock
6 Lighthunter; 20(t) violetkaipa; 22(t) Eric Isselee; 27(b) Denis and Yulia Pogostins; 29(b) Eric Isselee; 33(b) HomeStudio; 36(t) Jose AS Reyes; 47; 62 Dudarev Mikhail; 63 Abramova Kseniya; 65(t) haveseen; 70(t) Subbotina Anna; 73(b) Andrew Buckin; 75(t) Vladimir Wrangel, (c) SiberianLena, (b) Golden Pixels LLC; 76(b) Steve Design; 78 Madlen; 79(t) Vishnevskiy Vasily, (b) Christopher Halloran; 80(t) Oleg Zhevelev, (b) loskutnikov; 82(c) terekhov igor; 83(bl) jojof, (bc) RoJo Images, (br) aabeele; 84(b) Vilainecrevette; 86(t) Valentyn Volkov, (b) michaeljung; 87(l) Kbiros, (r) Smileus; 89(br) photka; 90 Eric Isselee; 93(t) I love photo; 94(t) maxstockphoto, (c) Krasowit; 96(c) Atlaspix; 97(c) Vishnevskiy Vasily; 98(c) Sergieiev; 101(tl) Borislav Borisov; 101(bc) Mark William Penny; 105(tl) viewgene; 106(r) Yurchyks; 108(c) R.A.R. de Bruijn Holding BV; 111(t) Pavel Vakhrushev; 115(tl) marilyn barbone, (tr) ULKASTUDIO; 117(tl) infografick; 121 Vitaly Titov; 122(l) John Carnemolla, (r); 123(b) MaszaS; 124(c) Joellen Armstrong, (tr) tale; 126(t) Hurst Photo, (b) Elena Schweitzer; 127(cr) Yasonya; 128(l) Eric Isselee, (r) BestPhotoPlus; 129(b) OmniArt; 130(t) Laborant; 131(t) Sandra van der Steen, (b) Lucie Lang; 132(c) Andrew Mayovskyy; 133(t) sevenke, (c) Hurst Photo, (b) Nattika; 135(c) Mirek Srb; 137(c) Elena Schweitzer; 139(t) Stanislav Fridkin, (c) Andreas Poertner, (b) Daxiao Productions; 140(b) fivespots; 142(t) Jim Barber; 143(cr) ssuaphotos; 144(tl); 145(t) Fotokostic; 146(r) Eric Isselee; 148(t) charles taylor; 149(b) design36; 152(r) Robyn Mackenzie; 153(t) Miramiska; 157(t) Nadezda; 158(t) SergiyN, (b) Brandelet; 159(b) Tomasz Trojanowski; 161(t) Kletr, (cr) Galushko Sergey; 163(b) Aleksandra Duda; 164(b) Palto, (t); 165; 168(t) Franck Boston, (b) S-F; 176(t) Dionisvera, (b) ZouZou; 179(t) Gelpi JM; 182(b) Beata Becla; 185(b) irin-k; 186(b)

All other photographs are from: digitalSTOCK, digitalvision, Dreamstime, Fotolia, iStockphoto, John Foxx, NASA, PhotoAlto, PhotoDisc, PhotoEssentials, PhotoPro, Shutterstock, Stockbyte

All artwork from the Miles Kelly Artwork Bank

Every effort has been made to acknowledge the source and copyright holder of each picture. Miles Kelly Publishing apologizes for any unintentional errors or omissions.